Create Your
DREAM
Classroom

Save Your Sanity, Escape the Rut, Sharpen Your Skills

Linda Kardamis

Table of Contents

To all the administrators, teachers, and professors from whom
I've learned these valuable lessons.

Acknowledgments

I praise God for working in my life and guiding me in this project. To Him be all the glory, for without Him I can do nothing.

To the administration, faculty, and staff at Cornerstone Christian Academy, thank you for being an incredible family of friends and mentors. I will be eternally grateful for the difference you made in my personal, spiritual, and professional life. In particular, thank you to Dan Buell, Bill Blankschaen, Sandi Ortiz, and Bernadette Bileci for your guidance and leadership.

Thank you to Tim, my incredible husband, for not only believing in and encouraging me as I wrote this book but also for creating the wonderful cover art.

Special thanks to my editor Dustin Brady for finding ways to make every lesson sound better.

To all my reviewers and proofreaders, I am extremely thankful. Rick Scarfi, Patricia Fisher, Vicky Hatfield, Beth Zapsic, Carol Carney, Kate O'Brien, Diana Harness, Julia Harris, Bethany Spears, Sandi Scarfi, Sharon Grammer, and Janet Blackstone, without you this book would not be what it is.

A Note from the Author

All I ever wanted to be was a teacher. I had dreamed about it for years and was smiling ear to ear when I finally stood in front of my first classroom of students. During that first year, people would ask me how things were going, and I would reply that things were good. In my heart, though, I knew that they weren't good, not really. I felt like I was just surviving, and I wanted to do way more than that. I wanted to thrive. My dream was to be a teacher, but I didn't feel like I was teaching in my dream classroom. Some days, it felt more like a nightmare.

I praise the Lord that He led me to an incredible school where I learned so much more than I taught. My administrators and fellow teachers were full of wisdom and practical advice, and I found myself growing as a teacher and as an individual. Over the summer, I spent a lot of time reading, reevaluating, and planning for the next year. When August came, I was prepared; and while I still made mistakes, the change in my classroom was incredible.

Every year I sought to reevaluate and grow, and as a result, I soon found myself where I wanted to be – teaching in my dream classroom. You can do the same thing. This book is designed to help you examine your own teaching and learn how to improve. The lessons will give you specific principles, strategies, and tips to help you create the classroom you've always wanted.

Some of you are picking up this book in the middle of a hectic year, while others are enjoying the relative calm of summer. To address the needs of both in-school and out-of-school teachers, I've divided some of the activities in this book to give more personalized direction.

If your school year is about to start, please begin with our Back-to-School Power Pack on page 135. The start of school provides an incredible opportunity to reinvent your entire classroom culture, and this section will prepare you to have the biggest impact during the first few weeks.

For the rest of you, I recommend starting at the beginning and working through each lesson. If you reach August and are still not finished, jump to the Power Pack. You'll get the most out of this book by following these three suggestions:

1. **Use the journal.** Most lessons include a journal prompt. You may be tempted to skip journaling to save time, but the process of writing down your thoughts will help you explore the concepts more deeply, remember what you learn, and develop a personalized action plan to make your classroom amazing. The experts agree that writing is a powerful process with incredible benefits.

   "When you write down your ideas you automatically focus your full attention on them." – Michael Lebouef

   "Write down the thoughts of the moment. Those that come unsought for are commonly the most valuable." –Francis Bacon, Sr.

   "Since I've started to write things down more often I have also noticed when reviewing old notes how much my memory can leak. The memory isn't very reliable." – Henrik Edberg

2. Interact. Connect with other teachers by participating in online discussions and joining our Facebook group, Christian Teachers' Lounge. It's the perfect place to share ideas, advice, and encouragement.

3. Read one at a time. Reading one selection at a time (rather than cramming them all together) allows you to process what you've learned and figure out how to best apply the principles to your own classroom.

These strategies are lessons I've learned through interactions with instructors, administration, and fellow teachers. I'm eternally grateful for those who have shared them with me and am excited for you to learn from them as well.

You also won't want to miss the special bonuses I've prepared just for *Create Your Dream Classroom* readers. Go to **teach4theheart.com/bonus** to access your free bonus pack.

Don't Miss Your Free Bonuses

I've prepared a list of bonus resources for you to help you implement the strategies discussed in this book. This includes printable discipline essays and class welcome sheets, additional articles that delve deeper into certain topics, and more.

These bonuses are just for readers of *Create Your Dream Classroom*. And they're absolutely free.

To access your free bonus pack, go to **teach4theheart.com/bonuses.**

Lesson 1:
Imagine Your Dream Classroom

As you're emailing parents, grading papers, and counseling students, you may start to lose sight of the big picture amid the details. But today you've picked up this book, so pause and think. *Is this the classroom you want to teach in?*

Maybe things are actually going pretty well or maybe you feel like you're about to drown. Either way, you're reading this book because you know your classroom can always be better. The title of this book is *Create Your Dream Classroom*, and that's exactly what you are going to do.

Take a minute to imagine what your ideal classroom would look like – the room where every student is listening, engaged, and happy, where you have zero discipline problems, where every moment is spent on task, where pigs fly and the moon is blue and...Okay, so we all know that no classroom will ever be perfect, but I'm serious about imagining your dream classroom. What would it look like? What would take place? How would you feel if you taught there every day?

You've got to think big. If the best you can imagine is a mediocre classroom, that's the best you'll ever achieve. In his book *Platform*, Michael Hyatt discusses the importance of big dreams. He claims,

"Thinking big is not a gift but a skill," and explains that you must take time to let your imagination roam wild with the possibilities. Then, you must write down your dream. "Wonderful things happen when you commit something to writing," he stresses. We are going to examine various aspects of teaching to help you hone your skills and create your dream classroom. But first, you have to know where you're heading.

You may have gone through some rough moments that have you feeling discouraged or frustrated. If you're not even able to imagine an amazing classroom right now, take a few minutes to vent your frustrations. Get out your journal and write down all the things that are discouraging you – anything and everything about yourself, others, the system, etc. Writing your frustrations will help get them off your chest and may even be quite therapeutic. Once they're down, you can let them go and move on with a clear mind to imagining how you'd like things to be different.

Journal: Imagine your dream classroom. What would be different from your current classroom? What would be the same?

Connect: Share your dream classroom with fellow teachers on our discussion page at teach4theheart.com/discussions.

Lesson 2:
A Fresh Start or Mid-Game Rally

Yesterday you imagined your dream classroom, but you may be seriously doubting if you'll ever be able to create such a room.

During my first year of teaching, I had plenty of doubts too. I made a lot of rookie mistakes that first year, and, as a result, my classroom was a bit of a mess. I remember vainly attempting to go over homework when half the students hadn't even done the assignment, another third of the class was having their own private conversations, and a boy in the back row was shooting a jump shot with his trash.

Not good.

By the second semester, however, I had learned some lessons and was trying to bring my classroom back under control. Unfortunately, changing things in the middle of the year is an uphill battle. I made some progress but was still not where I wanted to be.

That summer, I read *The First Days of School* by Harry Wong, in which he explains how the first days of school determine success for the whole year. I created a game plan for starting the year right, and when classes began in the fall, I implemented my new plan starting on day one. The results were incredible – an ordered classroom, on-task students, and a happy teacher. Things weren't perfect, and

I still had a lot to learn, but how refreshing the improvements were! If you're in the same boat I was, you can experience the same transformation.

One of the best aspects of teaching is that each year is a fresh start that allows you to reinvent your classroom culture. Even if last year's classroom was a disaster, this year's can still be fantastic. The secret is taking full advantage of the first week of school.

If you're picking up this book in the middle of the year, the transformation will be a two-step process. You'll make some changes as you read and implement others next fall. As you decide when to make your adjustments, keep these principles in mind:

1. **Make the most important changes now.** When you come across a principle that you know will improve your teaching, put it into practice as soon as possible. Changing mid-year may be challenging, but it's much better to embrace the challenge than to struggle for the rest of the year.

2. **Realize the changes you make this year may be incomplete**. If you're trying to drastically change your classroom culture, you will make progress, but you may not reach your destination this year. That's okay. You'll learn a lot through the experience and will be able to complete the transformation when you start a new school year.

3. **Keep a list of changes you plan to make next year**. As you read, you'll find some ideas that won't fit into your current classroom or would be too difficult to implement mid-year. Keep a list of all these changes so you'll have them ready to go for next year.

4. **Reevaluate over the summer and use the first week of school to your full advantage**. Next year, be prepared to take advantage of the clean slate and consistently implement your new policies and procedures the first week of school.

What about those of you who don't need a drastic transformation? What if your classroom is already running well? I love Lloyd Irvin's quote, "If you're not moving forward towards your goals, you are moving backwards. There is no standing still." This statement is as true in the classroom as it is in life. If we stop improving our teaching, it becomes stale and less effective. A good teacher is always open to fresh ideas.

Journal: Are you ready to make the changes necessary to create your dream classroom? What fears or attitudes may be holding you back? How can you overcome them?

> **Summer:** As you read, develop a list of changes you want to make next year. This list will be essential in the fall to ensure you follow through on your good intentions. Start the list today by writing down all the ideas you've already been considering.

Connect: Veterans, share your encouraging stories in Christian Teachers' Lounge, our Facebook discussion group. I'm sure the rookies would love to hear how you got past your rough start and created a successful classroom.

Lesson 3:
Reflection

"The unexamined life is not worth living." Socrates understood the importance of taking time to pause and reflect. Often we're in such a hurry to *do* something that we never take the time to evaluate ourselves. When we stop and reflect, we are able to see things more clearly. We can gain encouragement from our successes and clearly identify areas that need improvement.

Reflection is an important habit to develop, and I challenge you to schedule it into your school year. Get out your calendar right now and designate periods of reflection, even if they're only a few minutes. We all know that if something isn't intentionally planned, it's probably not going to happen.

Today, we're scheduling a time of reflection. Stop for a few minutes to think about your year. What has worked well? What hasn't? Why?

Consider the things that have caused frustration or discouragement. Why have they happened? What can you do to avoid them? How do you want things to be different?

What about the highlights? Whether your year has been enjoyable or disastrous, you can pick out things that have gone well. You have seen some success, and you have learned some lessons.

If you can't remember many successes, don't be discouraged. Growth takes time, both in yourself and in your students. And seeing growth in our students is often a multi-year process. I remember one student in particular who was quite challenging (to put it kindly). Basically, she used any form of antagonism or passive aggression that she could get away with. Her attitude was on display in various forms, including bumping into me every chance she got. Or, we would be in the middle of discussing why she was not allowed to write a poem about a toilet, and she would just walk away mid sentence. Later, during chapel, I would look back to find her sprawled across an entire pew. By June, I was about done. But midway through the next year, something changed. I noticed less and less attitude, and I soon realized I hadn't had a problem with her in weeks. Before long, she was smiling, respectful, and happy to come by my room just to talk. By our third year together, she had matured enough to tell me, "I can't believe I acted like that. What was I thinking?" What a pleasure it is to see growth like this! Maybe you've experienced something similar with one of your trouble students, but if not, don't give up. This story was years in the making. The seeds you plant may not sprout overnight, but God will bring His increase.

Journal: Evaluate your teaching. What has gone well? What hasn't? What have you learned? How does your current classroom differ from your dream classroom? Identify the top three things that you most want to change.

Lesson 4:
Worldview

We all know that the Bible is a powerful book, able to restore hearts and transform lives. But I was amazed when I began to realize that the Bible has something to say about many areas that I had considered secular or neutral. Every subject – from music and art to math and history – has opposing views that are either biblical or unbiblical. All of these areas have undergirding philosophies that can be traced back to a worldview. When I realized that the Bible speaks truth that can be applied to every area of life, a new world of insight opened up to me, and my life has never been the same.

Since then, I have grown to realize how critical it is to have a strong biblical worldview to guide in all areas of life. One of the greatest gifts we can give to our students and parents is to teach them how to think biblically. We need to show them that the Bible is alive and relevant, not only in areas we think of as spiritual, but also in all aspects of life, academia, and society. Every time we get the chance, we must speak biblical truth and show students how the Bible relates to their lives. This should be done during class lessons as well as one-on-one in counseling or disciplining students.

So let's start to think beyond the standard Christian hallmarks. Most Christians know that the Bible refutes evolution and that America was founded on biblical principles, but the vast majority do not realize that worldviews clash in many other areas as well. I've heard parents say they don't mind sending their children to public schools because they talk to them about how evolution is wrong. I'm not here to judge a parent's choice, but we cannot be this naive as we make key decisions. If evolution were the only concept up for debate, then I think we'd all be in pretty good shape. Unfortunately, secular humanism is being preached in many classrooms in America, and unbiblical worldviews are shaping the curricula and interactions. Our adversary is much more subtle than we think, and he's making inroads in many areas of which parents are not even aware. As Christian teachers, we must push back against this trend by instilling biblical truths in our students so that they can discern between truth and error. What a sobering task, but what an awesome opportunity!

If you teach in a non-Christian school, you can still teach students from a biblical worldview. Of course, you may not always be able to be as clear and obvious as you would like, but you can still weave biblical truths and principles into your lessons and interactions with students. God's truths are universal and powerful, even if the students aren't told they are coming from Scripture. Most public school systems are actively trying to teach secular humanism, but you have the opportunity and responsibility to push back against the darkness and give your students truth.

If this concept of a biblical worldview is new to you, pick up a copy of *The Universe Next Door* by James Sire or *Understanding the Times* by David Noebel. Both of these books provide great introductions to various worldviews and demonstrate how these views are shaping the world around us. If you don't have time to read these books during the year, put a reminder in your calendar to pick them up at the start of the summer.

Journal: What does a biblical worldview mean to you? How can you instill God's truths into your students through your lessons and daily interactions?

Lesson 5:
Whack a Mole?

Do you know the key to having a well-managed classroom? Deal with each infraction the first time it occurs. Don't let anything slide during the first few weeks of school.

My first year teaching, I created a nightmare by letting little things go. My intentions were good. I didn't want to whack students on the head right away for minor infractions such as whispering or getting up to throw something away. So I just didn't say anything, figuring it wasn't a huge deal. Soon, a few students were talking, others had their heads on their desks, and one was leaning back in his seat. *Still little things*, I thought. But the problems didn't stay small. The students quickly caught on that I wasn't dealing with anything, and the issues kept growing. Soon the majority of the class was chatting and laughing, and although the students weren't exactly swinging from the rafters, I got the sense that they felt like they could get away with it if they tried.

So what should I have done? I should have dealt with the very first infraction. My mistake was thinking that "dealing with" an issue means handing out a detention (or whatever discipline system your school uses). But that's where I was wrong. "Dealing with" simply means addressing the issue. I can say something as simple as, "Daniel, please do not whisper during class." That's it. That's the secret. I've addressed the issue, the class realizes that I have clear expectations, and the student doesn't feel humiliated or unjustly punished. (Of course if Daniel continues to whisper, I would have to do more, but during the first week of school that's normally all that's needed.)

Every single time a student doesn't meet your expectations during the first few weeks, you must address the infraction with a kind but firm statement. And I mean everything, even little things such as forgetting to take a hall pass. Later in the year you may not worry so much about all of this, but the first week is your chance to set the classroom culture for the rest of the year.

If you decide not to deal with minor issues at the beginning of the year, be aware that you'll have to deal with them at some point in the year. They will just escalate until they become major problems in a few months. That's the choice – deal with small issues early or big issues later.

So what do you do if you didn't start the year by addressing the small problems? The answer is to remember this principle going forward. Discuss each change you want to make with your class, then consistently address students **every time** they don't comply. Remember that if you're changing your expectations in the middle of the year, students will naturally need time to adjust. Don't punish them the first time they mess up. But do kindly and firmly remind them every single time they forget.

If you're facing major issues, I believe that the strategies in this book will be a great help to you. But don't wait until you finish this book to start making changes. Talk to a fellow teacher or administrator today for advice about how to get your classroom under control.

Journal: Did you address the small issues at the start of the year or did you wait until they escalated? What will you do differently?

Put it into practice: When I first had to correct students, I was extremely nervous and had to get up the nerve each time. If you feel the same way, practice your responses in front of the mirror. Practice until you're comfortable with what you are going to say and how you are going to handle each situation.

Lesson 6:
What's in a Name?

During my first year teaching middle school students, I found myself in a bit of a dilemma. When the bell rang, I knew that my class should be orderly, but it wasn't. In fact, it was often a disaster. I would have an activity on the board for students to complete, but no one did it. Instead, the class just kept chatting and laughing.

Some teachers have a natural air of authority and a voice that commands respect. I do not have those gifts. I cannot (and will not) raise my voice loud enough to be heard. In fact, I often struggle with losing my voice altogether. Moreover, I knew that even if I could get the students' attention that way, I wouldn't want to yell for class to come to order each day. The students knew this behavior was unacceptable, but since I didn't follow through with any discipline, they continued to talk. Making matters worse, I didn't know where to start. With half the class out of control, I wasn't about to give them all detentions.

I finally talked to my mentor teacher about the problem, and she gave me the following idea: When the bell rings, calmly walk to the board and start writing down the names of everyone who is talking. When the students notice, tell them that each student whose name is on the board now had a warning for talking. If those students speak out of turn again during the class period, they will receive discipline.

This seemed a bit juvenile to me, but I tried it, and wow did it work wonders! *The First Days of School* by Harry and Rosemary Wong explains how to make this method work on a regular basis. I tweaked their plan to fit my situation and soon had a surprisingly effective discipline tool. Here's how it works:

I start by explaining to my students (middle-school age) that if they are communicating in class without permission, they will receive a warning in the form of their name on the board. I take a few minutes to explain that this is not meant to embarrass them or make them feel like little kids, but as a way for me to give them a warning without stopping teaching. If a warned student talks again, I will give him another warning by putting a mark by his name. If he gets a third warning in the same class, he will receive a discipline essay. (In our school a detention is a very big deal, so I don't give a detention at this point. Depending on your situation, a detention or demerits may be appropriate.)

I watch carefully for the very first person who talks and give him a warning in the form of his name on the board. This shows right away that I mean what I say. When I give the first warning, I say something like, "Noah, you see I'm putting your name on the board. Remember that talking is not permitted and that this is just a warning to you that you were talking and that you need to stop. You are not in trouble at this point, but you will be if you continue to talk without permission." This shows the class that I am not demeaning the student and that he isn't yet in trouble but that he is being warned to correct his behavior. From then on, whenever a warning needs to be given, I simply walk to the board and write down the name. The student gets warned, the incorrect behavior stops, and I don't have to interrupt the flow of my teaching.

So what happens when I write names on the board? The level of talking decreases dramatically, students are more focused, and I am less flustered. In addition, I find that I hardly ever actually have to give out discipline. I probably give out essays for talking ten to fifteen times in an entire year. Please note, however, that you do need to be ready to hand out penalties when students get too many warnings. Otherwise, your class will quickly see that you don't mean what you say.

I found that this method has made the biggest difference at the start of class. There would still be days when the bell would ring and half the class would still be talking, but instead of allowing my stress level to rise, I would calmly walk to the board and start writing names. It didn't matter if I got everyone because it normally only took three or four names for the class to notice, quiet down, and get to work. What a better option that is than yelling!

The obvious downside to this method is that it seems juvenile. Elementary teachers, you have no problem there. I was a little nervous about using it in middle school at first, but I couldn't believe how well it works! High school teachers, I didn't use this method when I taught 11th and 12th graders, but it would still work if you needed it to. Personally, I would only use it in high school to correct an issue that is not being resolved by other methods.

Journal: If you think this method may be helpful for you, plan how you will use it. What infractions will result in a warning? How many warnings will you give before a student receives a penalty? What will the punishment be? How will you explain this method to your students?

Put it into practice: Once you have your plan in place, explain the new system to your students. Then, enforce it consistently for at least a few weeks. After that, you may find that you need to use it less and less.

Lesson 7:
When Frustrations Abound

One of the first verses young children learn is Ephesians 4:32, "And be ye kind one to another, tenderhearted, forgiving one another, even as God for Christ's sake hath forgiven you." We all want our students to practice this verse, but when the students are driving us crazy and their latest antics are the last straw, this verse can be difficult to follow ourselves.

Kindness should always be a hallmark of a Christian teacher, especially when we have to discipline students. No matter how frustrated we are, we can never lose our temper and yell at a student. When we do, we lose credibility and become the star of a funny story those students will tell for years to come. We cannot effectively disciple students in this way. It simply doesn't result in their learning the lesson we are trying to teach.

When we are frustrated and maybe even angry, we have to take time to calm down before speaking to the student. If necessary, tell him that you'll talk to him later. You can even send him out into the hall or to the principal's office if needed. He'll know he's in trouble, and you can take the time to get in the right frame of mind.

When it comes time to speak to the student, speak to him respectfully and kindly while also being firm. Explain why his actions were wrong and administer consequences if necessary. All of this is much more effective if done in a quiet, controlled manner than through yelling and screaming. When we admonish students in love, we follow the biblical model and become an example to our students instead of frustrating them or turning them off.

I love the phrase "speaking the truth in love" from Ephesians 4:15. Both parts are necessary – truth and love. We cannot claim to love our students without speaking truth to them; neither should we speak the truth without using a loving manner. When we put the two together, we can effectively disciple students and help them become the men and women God wants them to be.

Journal: Have you made a habit of being kind to your students or do you tend to lose your temper quite often? Pray about how God would have you change. Write down your goals.

Connect: Share your challenges, thoughts, and advice on our discipline discussion page at teach4theheart.com/discussions.

Lesson 8:
Seek First to Understand

In *The 7 Habits of Highly Effective People*, Stephen Covey teaches this principle: Seek first to understand, then to be understood. What an invaluable piece of advice for us to remember when disciplining and discipling students!

Often we teachers think of discipline as a lecture. We tell the student what he did wrong, what he should've done, and what punishment he will be receiving. But if we want to make a lasting impact and help the student grow, we need to first understand where he is coming from. So, ask the student what's going on and wait for him to respond. Listen carefully and try to understand what he is saying. You may find that there's been a misunderstanding. Or, you may discover that the student has a very unbiblical view of the situation. Whatever you hear will help you frame your response and enable you to speak to the student's heart instead of just giving the standard lecture.

Listening to students has helped me time and time again to determine how to proceed. I remember speaking one time with a seventh grader who had been giving several teachers a hard time. I asked her what was really going on and continued to gently probe until she started to open up. She told me how her old boyfriend had come to youth group the past week with a new girl on his arm. She was crushed and couldn't stop thinking about it. Of course, I had a lot to say to her about this. There were so many areas in which she was not thinking or acting biblically. But I would never have been able to address the real issues with her if I hadn't first taken the time to try to understand what she was thinking.

There's no way around it; listening takes time. Handing out punishment or reciting a few lines is fast and easy, but it will never produce lasting results, change a heart, or bring a student closer to Jesus. You can't have a half-hour conversation every time a student talks in class, but you should start looking for opportunities to really disciple your students. The time you invest will be well worth the sacrifice in eternity. That's why we're teachers in the first place, isn't it?

Journal: Do you seek to understand before trying to get your own point across? How can you apply this principle in your classroom?

Lesson 9:
Don't Charge a Gray Hill

"Don't charge a gray hill," my principal Bill Blankschaen replied when I asked him what I should do about a student I suspected was copying a friend's homework. At first I wasn't sure what I thought of this answer, but slowly the meaning and wisdom became clear. If you defend or attack a matter before you have clarity, you risk harming relationships only to find yourself the victor of an argument that doesn't even matter. While this principle applies in many areas, we're going to examine it in the realm of discipline.

There will be times when you are not exactly sure what happened, just as I was unsure whether or not the student was copying homework. We are often not really sure how to handle these situations or if the student should be punished. At this point, we have several choices:

1. **Punish the student you think is at fault.** This mistake has been made over and over by well-intentioned teachers. Maybe you have done this yourself, or maybe you or your child has been on the receiving end of undeserved discipline. Unjust punishment will severely damage the teacher/student relationship and can cause a multitude of problems. When a teacher does this, he is charging a gray hill, enduring casualties when the battle he's fighting isn't even a clear conflict. If this has been your habit, please reconsider.

2. **Put on your detective hat and conduct a thorough investigation.** Sometimes, you can figure out everything with a few well-placed questions to the right students. Other times, you realize you're not going to learn what happened without conducting a long investigation that will put students in difficult situations. And you still probably won't get to the bottom of it. When you have a situation like this, the investigation is probably not worth the time and will likely do more harm than good.

3. **Ignore the situation.** Although doing nothing is sometimes the best course of action, we teachers normally do nothing because we either don't know what to do or are just too busy. We cannot give in to the temptation to do nothing because it's easy, since this can cause students to feel like their behavior was acceptable or that they've gotten away with wrong. Don't feel that you have to do nothing – I've got one more option for you.

4. **Speak truth to the students but reserve punishment.** This gray hill is not worth charging, but it is worth addressing. Speak to the students you think may be involved and explain to them the truth. Tell them that you don't know exactly what happened but God does. If they weren't involved, then they don't have to worry about anything, but if they were, God saw and He knows. Explain to them again what the correct behavior should have been and what they should all do in the future if the situation arises again.

You may worry that a student is getting away with something, but you don't need to be concerned about this. The beauty of the situation is that one of two things will happen:

1. **The student will learn his lesson and correct his behavior.** If this happens, you've accomplished your goal.

2. **The student will not learn his lesson and will repeat the wrong behavior.** In this case, you will be watching him and aware of the potential problem. The hill will likely no longer be gray and you will no longer give him the benefit of the doubt. There can be no question that you have been more than fair when you administer the appropriate consequences.

Journal: What "gray hill" situations have you faced? How did you handle them? In hindsight, should you have handled any of them differently? How?

Lesson 10:
Iron Sharpens Iron

Proverbs 27:17 states, "As iron sharpens iron, So a man sharpens the countenance of his friend." Having master teachers as friends and mentors will sharpen your skills and help you become the best teacher you can be.

When I was a rookie teacher, I had a lot to learn. Questions came up every day, and I am extremely thankful for the help and guidance of my fellow teachers. Without their sound advice, I would not have grown nearly as much or as quickly. Over the years, their friendship and mentorship has been an incredible source of help and encouragement. We have laughed together, cried together, brainstormed together, and grown together. The teachers at my school have been great friends and mentors, full of biblical and practical wisdom. But what do you do if this is not the norm at your school?

Whether or not your school is full of master teachers who apply biblical principles to all they do, it is important for you to seek out wise, godly colleagues. Identify teachers whom you admire both as a teacher and as a person. It's great if you have at least one or two of these teachers at your school, but if not, look for them in your church, social circles or our online discussion group. Then be intentional about spending time with them. Maybe instead of locking yourself in your room to grade papers during lunch, you should head to the lounge and eat with those teachers. The encouragement and exchange of ideas over lunch can be invaluable.

You should also be intentional about scheduling coffee or lunch with these teachers. The summer is a great time to discuss ideas away from the stress and pressure of school. Create a list of questions you may have and ask colleagues their thoughts and opinions. You'll be amazed at the synergy that can result from these conversations. Remember, iron sharpens iron.

Veterans, you can be a great blessing to new teachers by intentionally mentoring them. Invite them to eat with you, share with them the lessons you've learned, and encourage them during the rough days.

Journal: What teachers do you know that you admire and are of like mind? Plan how you can build relationships with these teachers.

Put it into practice (summer): Contact at least one or two of these teachers and ask to schedule lunch or coffee later in the summer. Getting a date on both of your calendars will keep it from becoming a "we should get together sometime" nonevent.

Put it into practice (school year): Plan at least one day this week to connect with another great teacher. Also, put a note in your calendar to contact at least one or two of these teachers in May and ask them to plan a time for lunch or coffee over the summer.

Lesson 11:
Where's the Line?

Mr. Sanders, attired in skinny jeans and Hollister polo, high fives a group of freshmen as he hurries toward his geometry class. "All right, all right, let's get going!" he shouts jovially as the students mosey away from their conversations and into their seats. "So what's the news!?" he asks. "Dan, what did you and the guys do last weekend?" As Dan launches into a hilarious story about a prank they pulled on their soccer coach, the girls giggle and whisper. Ten minutes into the class period, the story concludes. "Dude, that's awesome!" the teacher replies. "These are the days! I've got a great story for you, but we've got to start our lesson for today. I'll come tell you at lunch."

If you're like me, you're cringing as you read this scenario. You know that this teacher is going to have a hard time being effective and that, while the students may like him, they probably do not respect him. We can easily recognize Mr. Sanders's unprofessionalism because it is so blatant, but we must honestly evaluate if we've let a little unprofessionalism sneak into our own classrooms.

One of the biggest downfalls of teachers (especially younger ones) is giving in to the desire to be liked by our students. I hope none of us will come close to Mr. Sanders's extreme behavior. But if we desire to be friends with our students, we will act unprofessionally and fall prey to some of the same dangers. Everyone wants to be liked, but if you let this desire affect your decisions, you will not be a successful teacher. Ironically, your students may not even end up liking you that much. They certainly won't respect you. Maybe you are experiencing this, or maybe you've seen what it has done to other teachers. If this is an area in which you struggle, make a change now, starting with your attitude.

Balancing professionalism with caring relationships can sometimes be difficult, but its importance cannot be overstated. You should care about your students, but that doesn't mean that you have to act like their peer. You cannot see yourself as their friend if you're trying to be their mentor. You cannot act around your students the way you act around your own friends or the way you acted in high school or college.

Here's an example: Suppose as a female teacher, an 11th grade girl approaches you, excited to tell you that she just got asked out to the major upcoming event at your school. There are two ways you can respond:

> **Option 1:** Ahh!!! (insert squealing and jumping up and down) I knew he would ask you! Oh, you're going to be the cutest couple ever! What are you going to wear!? Is he going to pick you up!? This is the best thing ever!! (Okay, I really hope none of you would go that far, but you get the picture.)

> **Option 2:** Wow, Hailey, that's fantastic! I'm really happy for you. John seems like a great guy, and I know you'll have a fun time with him. Have you told your mom yet?

Being professional doesn't mean you're uncaring, distant, or boring. Option 2 shows the student that you care, while you maintain your role as a mentor as opposed to a friend (and, incidentally, encourage the parent/child relationship in the process).

If this is an area in which you know you need to improve, seek out the counsel of teachers whom you view as caring yet professional. Discuss with them your past interactions with students and ask them for advice about becoming more professional.

Journal: Evaluate your professionalism. Are there any areas in which you can improve?

Put it into practice (school year): If your professionalism has been lacking, change your demeanor starting today. For some, this will just be a mental change that will start manifesting itself in your interactions. Others, however, may need to talk to particular students and explain to them what the appropriate teacher-student relationship will look like going forward.

Connect: Join the conversation on our discussion page at teach4theheart.com/discussions.

Lesson 12:
What about Facebook?

In the last lesson we talked about professionalism, and today we'll address this in a specific area – Facebook. Are any of the students at your school your Facebook friends? If they are, you have a problem (although we'll make an exception for family members).

You may wonder if it's really a big deal, but this one mistake can severely undermine your professionalism. Why? Because you're not a teacher on Facebook – at least I'm not. When I started teaching, I had just graduated from college and gotten married. If someone had looked at my Facebook page, they would have seen a young college student and a newlywed who had just returned from her honeymoon. That was fine – for my friends. But not for my students. My students couldn't see me this way; they needed to see me as a competent teacher whom they could respect and learn from.

Could I be both the newlywed and the competent teacher? Of course. But kids have trouble seeing both sides. They don't need to see all your cruise vacation pictures, your rants about sports, your *LOLs* and emoticons. This brings you down to the level of friend instead of mentor. You'll have a chance to tell your students about yourself in a way that is both professional and personal, but Facebook is not that forum.

Students will request to be your friend on Facebook, but the best response is to simply tell them that you don't accept students as Facebook friends. If they ask why, explain to them that you value your relationship with them but that you're their teacher, not their friend. The students may or may not completely understand this, but they will come to respect you for it.

What about parents? The decision to accept parents as Facebook friends may not be quite as clear as the decision to accept students, but the same principles apply. You want to maintain a professional relationship with the parents of your students, and you are not a teacher on Facebook. Personally, I accept parents with whom I have a relationship outside of just being their child's teacher (a fellow teacher's wife, a fellow church member, etc.), but otherwise, I typically don't.

But what if you want to harness the power of social media to communicate with your students for your classroom, club, or sports team? We said before that you're not a teacher on Facebook, but if you do want to use social media to communicate with students, create a separate profile in which you **are** a teacher. Your username would be "Mr. Smith," your profile picture a professional headshot, and every interaction you make would be strategic and professional. Having a profile like this could open up a world of opportunity, but it still requires caution. Constantly ask yourself, "Is this professional?" If there's even a slight doubt, don't do it. Be very cautious about commenting on students' pictures or statuses. Instead, think about creating a group or a page through which your communication takes place.

Put it into practice: If you have any students as Facebook friends, go through your Facebook account today and defriend them. You may want to message them first or say something to them in person so that they understand why you are defriending them. You could say something such as "Because I value the professional relationship between myself and my students, I have decided to no longer have any of my students as Facebook friends. Please realize this is not a personal slight, but that I value our working relationship and want to protect it."

Lesson 13:
The Power of Prayer

Do you ever stop to think how amazing it is that we can pray? The Almighty God cares about our every request, longing, hope, and sorrow. How incredible that is! Yet, I know I often struggle with spending time in prayer. I don't know why. Maybe it's because my mind is always going a mile a minute with to-do lists, and I have trouble making myself stop and be still. Maybe you struggle with prayer as well, or maybe it's a strong area for you. Either way, prayer is important – probably more important than anything else we can do.

We all know that prayer is essential, but it's so easy to forget. A few years ago, one of my administrators shared with us a concept popularized by Stephen Covey: "Do what is important, not necessarily urgent." This resonated with me. Prayer doesn't feel urgent. There are a million things pressing down on us all the time. But it is very important, so we need to be intentional about including it in our day.

A few of our lessons will set aside time for prayer, and today the focus is on praying for your administration. Whether your administrators are the best in the world or are driving you crazy, praying for them is important. They are constantly making decisions that impact you, your classroom, your students, and your school. They face more challenges and obstacles than we realize, and they need wisdom to make the right decisions.

So pause today and pray for them. Pray that God will guide their thoughts and actions. Ask Him to work in your school according to His plan and for His glory. Even if your school is not a Christian school, you should still pray for your administration. God can work even through unsaved administrators to accomplish His purpose for you and your students.

Some of you may like to journal your prayers. I have found that this helps me concentrate, and maybe you will find it helpful as well.

Put it into practice/Journal: Pause right now and pray for the administration at your school. Pray specifically regarding any areas about which you are frustrated or concerned. Allow God's peace to fill you as you pray.

Connect: Share your prayer requests in Christian Teachers' Lounge. If you haven't found us yet, search for Christian Teachers' Lounge group on Facebook and request to join.

Lesson 14:
If the Parent Asks

During my student teaching internship, Dr. Phyllis Rand, the Dean of Education, posed the following question to us: A parent comes to you concerned about his child's work. He asks you to give him a report each week detailing his child's progress. What do you say?

My immediate response as an eager education student was that of course I should say yes. Shouldn't I do everything I can to help my students? While I can still appreciate my own enthusiasm, it only took a few months of teaching to see why a teacher may be tempted to give the opposite answer. *No, I can't do that. I have over 100 students to keep track of, and I don't have time for all this correspondence!*

But neither of these responses was the answer my professor gave. The best answer? Promise a report, but give the responsibility back to the parent. You see, if you promise to email him every week and forget even one time, you have broken your promise. But if the parent is responsible for starting the conversation, you don't have to worry about making a promise you can't keep. So what do you say? Something like, "Mr. Adams, I think that's a great idea. Why don't you email me (or call me) each week asking for an update on Clarissa's progress, and I'll be happy to respond with a report."

Over the years, I have been incredibly thankful for this gem of wisdom, as it has saved me many times from committing myself to something I cannot fulfill. I've found three specific benefits of using this approach:

1. **You are still able to help the parent and student.** As teachers, we should be invested enough in our students that we want to take the necessary time to communicate with parents. But for those of us with 100 or more students, the requests parents make can sometimes be impossible to keep up with. This response shows that we care enough about the student to take the time to give a report when it's requested.

2. **It's not overwhelming to you.** Despite my best intentions, I forget things sometimes, and I know you do, too. If I had promised to send a weekly report, I would have forgotten at least once. We should never make promises we can't keep. With this approach, the only thing you have to do is respond to an email when you receive one.

3. **The parent is responsible**. According to the Bible, parents are the ones who are primarily responsible for their children. This response puts the responsibility back where it should be – with the parents.

Most of the time, parents are happy with this answer. Sometimes I will get one or two inquiring emails, but they normally don't keep coming. And that's fine. If the parent isn't remembering to send the emails, then it's not important enough to them for you to devote your valuable time to a weekly report. If something comes up that deserves the parents' attention, of course you should already be contacting them about it.

I did have one parent, however, that didn't like my answer. She replied that if she had to remember to ask for the report, she would probably forget. I kindly but honestly explained why I was giving the responsibility back to her. She still wasn't thrilled about the idea because she didn't want the responsibility, but that's okay. You don't have to give in to parents who are overly insistent. Kindly show them you care about them and their student, but don't let them guilt you into overextending yourself. If they're not willing to make the effort to initiate contact, it's not truly important enough to them.

One disclaimer: There may be special situations that warrant your direct intervention and for which you may need to take the responsibility to send weekly or even daily reports. I would still, however, be careful about the promises I make. Something like "I'll send you reports as often as possible" is a promise we know we can keep.

Journal: Have you been asked by parents to provide updates like these? How did you handle the request? What will you say if you receive similar requests in the future?

Lesson 15:
Expect the Expected

In *The First Days of School,* Harry and Rosemary Wong describe a well-managed classroom as a "predictable environment" in which the students know what is expected of them. As such, two of our greatest allies as teachers are procedures and routines. Build your predictable environment with procedures for every area of your classroom, from passing in papers to reviewing homework to conducting restroom breaks.

If you try to run your classroom without procedures, you will waste a lot of time, add unnecessary confusion, and cause more discipline issues. On the other hand, if you spend just a little time developing your classroom procedures now, you will become much more efficient for the rest of the year.

Procedures don't need to be fancy, but they do need to be carefully thought through. Let's take, for example, a procedure for students who need a tissue during class. You could allow students to stand up and get a tissue without asking, require them to raise their hand so you can bring them a tissue, require them to raise their hand so you can give them permission to get one themselves, or ask them to raise their hand with the other hand over their nose as a signal so you can just nod permission without interrupting class. Think through what is the best method for your classroom, carefully weighing the pros and cons of each option. Secondary teachers may even have separate procedures for different grades. Maybe 7th graders have to ask permission but 12th graders can get a tissue on their own. Something as small as getting tissues may seem unimportant, but if you've been teaching for long, you've seen how disruptive these minor issues can be. They don't have to be, though, if you have good procedures.

Put it into practice (summer): Think through a typical day and go through the list below to make sure you have a procedure in place for each area. Write down any new procedures. Don't forget to think through the details as well. When determining a procedure for how you'll grade papers in class, you can't just think, "We'll exchange and grade." There are so many details to consider. How will the students exchange? What writing utensils will they use to grade? Will you take questions? Should students write in the correct answer? How will the assignments be scored? Should the grader sign his name? The more details you consider ahead of time, the smoother your first week of school will go.

Put it into practice (school year): During the school year, you likely already have many procedures established. Take some time today to rethink your routines. Go through the list below and determine if there are any procedures you would like to change. Make one list of changes you want to make right away (We'll discuss the best way to implement these new procedures in the next lesson). Add any changes that you want to make at the start of next year to your ongoing list.

Areas to consider:

1. Restroom breaks (elementary)
2. Classroom helpers
3. Passing in papers
4. Grading papers
5. Hall passes
6. Getting a tissue
7. Starting class
8. Going over homework
9. Giving homework assignment
10. Turning in late work
11. Communicating work when a student is absent
12. Making up tests/quizzes when a student is absent
13. Taking notes
14. Lining up (elementary)
15. Ending class
16. Fire drills/other emergency drills
17. Coming into class late (teach students what to do when they're tardy)
18. Preparing for tests/quizzes
19. Turning in tests/quizzes
20. Group projects
21. What to do if the teacher isn't there
22. Anything else you do in your classroom

If there's an area in which you are unsure or have been struggling, ask another teacher for help or post the question on our discussion page at teach4theheart.com/discussions.

Lesson 16:
Practice Makes Perfect

I'm sure you have heard the saying "practice makes perfect." This phrase clearly applies to procedures in your classroom – well, sort of. We'll get to that in a minute.

When you implement a new procedure, it is not enough to simply tell your students what you expect of them. You have to practice – and practice everything. This is especially true with elementary and middle school students, but it's also applicable in high school. When teaching any procedure, always follow these four important steps:

1. **Give clear, specific directions.** The first time you tell your students to pass in papers, you cannot just say, "Please pass in your papers." If you do, you'll get some papers but also a lot of chaos. Be specific in your directions. Try something more like, "Now we are going to pass our papers in. Those at the back of the row will pass theirs forward first. Please wait to pass in your paper until you have the stack. When it gets to the front, Makenzie will pass them to Jared who will pass them to Steve who will give the whole pile to Alex. Alex, please place the stack on my desk."

2. **Have the students practice the procedure.** After you give the directions, have the students actually complete the task. As they do, watch to see if they are doing everything correctly.

3. **Kindly correct any piece of the process that is done incorrectly.** This is the most crucial element in teaching procedures because practice doesn't necessarily make perfect. If a basketball player practices foul shots with the wrong form, will he get better? Probably not. He needs a coach to correct his mistakes before he tries again. The same is true with your procedures. The chance that students will pass in the papers correctly the first time, despite your perfectly planned explanation, is about two percent. They'll get it mostly right, but Jon won't wait for the person behind him, Elana will put hers upside down, and Alex will forget what to do with the stack when he gets it. When you see mistakes, kindly remind your students the way you'd like to have it done.

4. **Have the student(s) redo the part of the process that was incorrect.** Yes, that's right. Redo it. It may seem like you're nit-picking at the time, but this is the step that will help your students remember how to follow the procedure correctly. The effort you invest during the first few days will save you lots of time and frustration the rest of the year.

A couple tips:

1. Be kind when you correct the students and don't make them feel stupid. Say things like, "I know it's a lot to remember, but…" or "Thanks you so much for _____; just don't forget to _____."

2. Plan to cover less material the first week of school so that you have time to teach and practice procedures. You might feel like you're wasting time, but you're not. The minutes you invest during the first week will save hours throughout the year.

Put it into practice (summer): Go back over your list of procedures and plan clear, specific directions for each one. Make notes as needed. Anticipate how you will respond when students need correction as they learn your procedures.

Put it into practice (school year): Go back over your list of procedures you want to change and think through clear, specific directions for each one. Then, start teaching your students these new procedures using the pattern above.

For more help with procedures, read *The First Days of School*. This excellent resource, in which many of these ideas are found, gives details for planning and implementing your procedures.

Lesson 17:
When the Bell Rings

The bell rings, but chaos reigns. A few students mosey to their seats while the rest of the class ignores the bell, still discussing last night's big game. Robin is frantically searching for her homework, Emma dashes into the room, and Tyler is trying to bum lunch money from his classmates.

Your classroom does not have to look like this. The start of class should be an orderly and productive time, but this will only happen if you plan your start-of-class procedures and diligently teach them to your students. In *The First Days of School*, Harry & Rosemary Wong explain that the key to order is starting each class with an assignment. Have a place where you write this activity each day and teach the students that when they arrive to class, they should start on it right away and stop talking when the bell rings.

An orderly start to class won't happen by accident. You will need to practice these procedures and consistently correct wrong behavior, either with verbal warnings or appropriate consequences.

Below is the start-of-class plan that I use in my middle school math classrooms. Yours will not look the same as mine, but this should give you an idea of the things you'll need to consider. (Elementary teachers: This is written specifically to address a middle school/high school issue, but these strategies can be easily adapted to elementary classroom transition times as well.)

When students enter the classroom, they have four tasks to accomplish (which I post on a sign in my room):

1. **Find their seats.** Students are not allowed to wander the room or congregate at friends' desks. When they enter the room, they are to go to their seat (unless they are accomplishing a classroom task).

2. **Get out their homework.** If you train your students to find their homework when they first sit down, you will save a lot of time and stress. Otherwise, the whole class will be waiting as one student frantically searches through his overflowing book bag.

3. **Clear their desks.** We'll discuss this in Lesson 33, but clear desks help prevent distractions.

4. **Start the bellwork.** I have a place on my whiteboard for the day's bellwork assignment. Bellwork varies depending on that day's activities. Typically, it is a practice exercise consisting of review problems, but on quiz/test days the bellwork is simply "prepare for quiz."

While students complete the bellwork, I am able to take attendance and speak with any students I need to connect with. If we have homework due that day, students are also putting the problems on the board for us to go over.

Things don't always go perfectly, but the more consistent I am with my expectations, the smoother they go. If the bell rings and students are still talking, I start writing names on the board (remember Lesson 6), and they quickly settle into their routine.

Journal: Evaluate how well your start-of-class procedures have worked. What can you do to improve them? Write your plans for the start of class and know exactly what you will expect from your students.

Put it into practice (school year): Once you decide on a new plan, you'll need to implement it. Teach your students the new procedures then check their progress, correcting as needed. If you're changing your procedure in the middle of the year, you may encounter some natural resistance, but that's okay. Just be patient and consistent, and your students will settle into their new routine quickly.

Connect: Have questions or advice? Join the conversation on our discussion page at teach4theheart.com/discussions.

Lesson 18:
Stuck Behind the Lectern

Where do you spend most of your time while teaching? When I was a student, my teachers stayed almost exclusively behind their lecterns, and I never really thought much about it. However, when I started observing master teachers during my education courses in college, I noticed that they rarely stayed in one place. They moved effortlessly around the classroom and were just as comfortable teaching from the back of the room as they were from the front. Their movement allowed them to better control their classroom and accomplish more in less time. If you find yourself stationary as you teach, why not consider some ways that moving around the classroom can help make you more effective:

1. **Move to a discipline problem.** If a student is off task, talking, or distracted, walk toward that student and teach from right next to his desk for a few minutes. You'll likely get his attention back without interrupting your flow of teaching. Even if you must directly address a student, walking toward him allows you to stop and whisper to him before continuing with the rest of your lesson. This is also a great way to check out a questionable situation.

2. **Move for variety.** Walking as you lecture provides variety for the students and allows you to better monitor how well they are tracking you. Once again, you won't interrupt the flow of your teaching while you make these assessments.

3. **Multitask.** Being comfortable moving around your room while you teach allows you to multitask better. Does a student need a Band-Aid? Keep teaching while you walk to your desk, find one, and hand it to him.

4. **Move around the room during work times**. When students are working silently, walk around the room. You will be able to answer questions and redirect students who are not focusing.

The first time you walk to the back of the room and continue your lecture from there, the students may give you an odd look. But it's good to keep students on their toes, and your classroom will become more interesting and efficient as a result.

Journal: How can breaking out from behind the lectern help improve your classroom?

Put it into practice (school year): This is an easy and fun method that you can try tomorrow. Just start moving around your classroom and see what you think.

Lesson 19:
The Last Page

Does finishing the textbook sound like an impossible task? It doesn't have to be. With careful planning and prioritizing, I was able to finish my curriculum every year, and you can too. Let's discuss some important principles to help you reach the last page:

1. **Manage your time wisely**. This one is obvious. The more time you waste, the less material you will cover; the more efficient you are, the more time you have to teach. We'll discuss specific time-saving tips in the next lesson.

2. **Prioritize**. You don't have to teach every lesson in the book to reach the last page. What you need to do, though, is prioritize which lessons and concepts are the most important and cover those. When you're behind, cut the less important sections in each chapter instead of the last fourth of the book.

3. **Plan ahead**. Before the school year starts, set up a rough calendar to plan when you will teach each chapter. If you've already started the year, create one as soon as possible. Predict as accurately as you can, but realize that this is just an estimate to help you know if you are on track throughout the year.

4. Constantly check and adjust to stay on track. Snow days, illness, school plays, and confused students will all conspire against your schedule. The key at this point, once again, is to prioritize. Look ahead and think, *what lessons/concepts are not as crucial to the course?* Then, either skip or shorten them to get yourself back on track with your calendar. If you constantly revise and adjust your lesson plans in this way, you'll reach that elusive last chapter.

5. Know when to spend extra time on a concept. Once again, prioritizing is key when deciding whether or not to spend extra time on a confusing lesson. If the concept is foundational to the entire course, an extra day or two (or even three) will be a good investment. If, however, the lesson isn't an essential building block, don't be afraid to move on. You have to balance your need to help struggling students with your responsibility to teach as much as you can to the brighter students.

Put it into practice: If you haven't already done so, create a rough calendar plan for each of your classes. See Appendix A for directions on how to set this up.

Lesson 20:
Time Savers

Did you know that if you waste just five minutes of each class period, you'll end up wasting an entire month of school? Considering how easy it is to waste five minutes, it's no wonder most teachers struggle to complete their curriculum. But this doesn't have to be your fate. Try some of these time-saving tricks to make the most of every minute:

1. **Use the magic words, "Ask me after class"** (or for elementary, a time when you're free, such as recess). Often students ask questions that lead to unhelpful rabbit trails. You don't have time to answer them during class, but you don't want to shut them down either. Just say, "Ask me after class." If they really care about the answer, they'll find you. I've found that about 95 percent of the time, students don't bother to ask the question on their own time.

2. **Have students do work for you.** Elementary teachers use this method all the time, but secondary teachers can try it too. Have students complete tasks such as recording attendance, taking notes for absent students, passing out papers, and filling out their own hall passes. I normally choose reliable, sharp students who typically finish their work early and give

them a task for about a month. They are then responsible to complete it each day without me reminding them.

3. **Review tests at the end of the period** (or for elementary, right before a sharp break such as recess, lunch, or a special class). Have you ever had students use half a period asking questions about a test, when you only budgeted five minutes? A better method is deciding how long you want to spend reviewing a test and stopping class that many minutes early. If students have more questions than you have time, they can ask them after class. Once again, you weed out questions that students don't really care about. I normally get through extra questions in just one or two minutes (plenty of time to start my next class without delay).

4. **Read answers quickly.** When reading answers for students to grade, move quickly. Some teachers think that if they read the answers slowly enough, students won't need as many repeated, but speaking slowly often just bores most of the students and rarely cuts down on repeats. If you start reading answers quickly, your students will soon learn to listen quickly as well.

5. **Use question marks when grading in class.** When students grade each other's papers in class, don't take questions. Instead, teach them to put a question mark next to any answers they're not sure are correct. You'll be amazed by the amount of time you save when you don't have to consider every possible answer on the spot.

6. **Give directions as you pass out papers.** Silently counting and passing out papers wastes so much time. Give directions or review while you pass out papers. You can also count them ahead of time and stagger them.

7. **Develop efficient procedures.** Procedures save time because they allow you to start tasks without explaining directions each time.

8. **Use class-response sayings to get attention.** I can't tell you how many times I've unsuccessfully flipped the lights, failing to regain my students' attention. If you find yourself wasting time trying to quiet your class, try a class-response saying. For example, if you say "ready to roll?" your whole class should respond "here we go!" [For more information about this strategy, check out Whole Brain Teaching.]

Journal: Will any of the above strategies help you save time in your classroom?

Connect: What other time-saving techniques do you use? Share them with fellow teachers on our discussion page at teach4theheart.com/discussions.

Lesson 21:
To Give or Not to Give

Bill Blankschaen argues that homework "robs us all of that most precious resource – time – and often gives nothing but hatred for learning in return."[1] While this view may seem extreme, it actually contains a lot of truth. Maybe it's time we teachers take a second look at the sacred cow of homework.

As a math teacher, I believe homework is a vital part of learning because students must practice the skills they learn in class. However, the school in which I taught was constantly urging us teachers to give less homework. While my first inclination was to be defensive, I soon saw the wisdom of this requirement.

We all want our students to have strong family relationships. As such, we need to value our students' time at home and think carefully about the work we ask them to complete during valuable family evening hours.

---

1. Bill Blankschaen, "Why Schools Should Get Rid of Almost All Homework," FaithWalkers. Sept. 7, 2012.

Now, believe me, I understand the arguments for homework. I've made them myself. If students would just use their class and study hall time wisely, they would have much less to do at home. I agree. But despite that, there are still some general homework principles we should be following as we strive to partner with families:

1. **Homework should be valuable.** How often do we really stop to think about whether or not the homework we assign is truly necessary? Sometimes, we just assign homework because we think we should or because there's a worksheet in the curriculum. Instead, stop and think about each assignment. Will the homework truly help students learn? Does this assignment have to be done at home or could we fit it into our class time? If the answer is yes and the assignment is critical to learning, then we do our students a disservice if we omit it. On the other hand, if we evaluate honestly and realize that the assignment is really just busywork, then we should value the students' time enough to eliminate it.

   I remember my 8th grade Bible teacher requiring us to color each page of our Bible notes with colored pencils. Yes, you read correctly. We were to creatively color each of the 50+ pages. The purpose? He wanted us to put so much time into the notes that we wouldn't throw them away when the year was done. This task epitomized time wasting and frustrated the class. Just because a teacher can think of a justification for an assignment doesn't mean that it's valuable enough to be assigned.

2. **Quality versus quantity**. One way to avoid overwhelming students while still helping them learn is focusing on quality versus quantity. I've seen students come home with two-page worksheets of math problems each night. I don't know

if the teacher realizes how long it takes them to complete those problems and how frustrating that can be. As a middle school math teacher, I know that practicing math is extremely important, but I asked myself, "What is the smallest number of problems I can assign to ensure that my students learn without overwhelming them?" I arrived at six or seven problems per assignment, enough that students get to practice each concept without feeling like they're starting an insurmountable task. I then focus on quality. I expect the students to try their absolute best on those few problems. My encouragement to you is to ask yourself the same question, "How can I boil this assignment down to its most crucial components?" Focus on quality assignments to make sure your students maximize their learning when they're away from class.

3. **Use every minute of class time.** Don't waste any class time and don't allow your students to either. You will find that some homework assignments can be completed during class (or at least started) if you are diligent about using your class time to its full advantage. I often give students the last 5-10 minutes of class to start their homework, and I walk around to make sure they are doing so. This also gives me a chance to help students and clarify the assignment.

Put it into practice: Honestly evaluate your own homework assignments. Maybe it would be wise to have another teacher analyze your homework with you. No teacher thinks he is giving too much homework, so it sometimes takes a colleague's fresh perspective to get a clear picture. Brainstorming ways to limit homework with other teachers can also be very helpful. I know that when I've had to limit my homework, my first reaction has always been to panic. But when I've thought it through, I've always found ways to make it work while keeping my academic expectations high.

Journal: Why do you assign homework? How do you determine what to assign? Can you limit the amount of homework you assign while still maximizing learning? Be creative.

Lesson 22:
Inspect What You Expect

My first year of teaching, I didn't collect homework. I walked around to make sure the students had completed the assignment, but that was it. As the year went on, my students' work grew progressively worse, until one day I received a set of half-worked problems on a torn sheet of computer paper. That day I had to face the fact that my method was not working. I was not adequately inspecting what I expected.

If you have an expectation but never check on your students to make sure they are following through, you can be sure they're not. You may have a handful of amazing students who will follow your every direction without any supervision, but that's not the norm. I was a motivated straight-A student in high school, but when my history teacher never asked if I read the assigned chapters, I stopped reading them after a few weeks.

We've got to find ways to make sure our students are doing what we ask them to do. The problem, though, is that we teachers are extremely busy. Our "free periods" are not coffee breaks. We're running frantically from task to task, and the last thing we have time for is grading every scrap of paper that our students complete. The good news is that you don't have to grade everything.

Wait, is that a contradiction? No. The key is to make sure your students realize that everything they do in class *could* be taken for a grade, even though it won't always be. Here are some tips to make this work:

1. **"Randomly" collect worksheets**, practice exercises, notes, and practice writings to take as a grade. I put *randomly* in quotes because you want the process to seem random to the students, even though you actually have it planned to your advantage. I typically grade classwork on days when the majority of the students are in class and most of the students finish the assignment. I normally do not grade work from days when the class is struggling to grasp a complex topic. But when the students ask if a worksheet is going to be graded, I always answer with a variation of, "It could be, so do your best."

2. **Have the students grade work in class** and count it as a very small grade. Allow students to put a question mark on the top if they think their paper was graded incorrectly, and don't take the time to regrade anything without a question mark. Just input the score into your gradebook. If these assignments are worth only a small percentage of your students' grades, grading mistakes won't really matter. This will save you time while keeping the students motivated.

3. **Collect papers even when you don't plan to grade them.** I've found that collecting work done in class makes a difference in quality, even if I never grade it. You can go over the answers in class and then ask the students to write the number wrong at the top and turn in the assignment. Your students will get the impression that you looked at the papers, even if all you

do is move the stack directly from your inbox to your outbox. You still need to grade some assignments, but you can collect and return a lot more than you have time to grade.

4. **Give short quizzes.** You can inspect students' notes by giving a short open-notes quiz the day before a test. Most students will love this, as they should do very well. This method also works effectively to check reading assignments. Just be sure to ask big-picture questions that the student should know if they read (as opposed to quizzing them on the details).

5. **Use class time to grade when appropriate.** I grade my students' class notes while they take their test. All I do is flip through them quickly to make sure they have the main ideas. I can get through all of them in one period and thus avoid carting around stacks of notebooks. When I started grading students' notes, their quality improved dramatically.

Remember that the key to having great effort in class is not to grade everything but for the students to know that every assignment *could* be collected and graded.

One last note: We've discussed strategies for inspecting class work, but don't forget to inspect the behaviors you expect as well.

Journal: How can you inspect your students' work without actually grading everything?

Lesson 23:
Grammar, Rhetoric & Logic

Anyone familiar with the classical model of education will recognize grammar, rhetoric, and logic as the trivium of classical education. While I have never taught in a classical school, I believe this model contains valuable insight for all teachers.

We all know that elementary students are very different from high schoolers, and that middle school carries its own set of challenges. We recognize that different procedures, expectations, and discipline policies are appropriate for each level. But academics should also be tailored to the age of the student, not just in their degree of difficulty, but also in their core focus.

Elementary: Elementary classrooms must focus on foundational building blocks of knowledge. Children can memorize facts and figures most easily, and they must learn the facts before reaching middle school. Some educators are pushing to eliminate this focus on drilling foundational truths like multiplication tables, but they're playing a dangerous game. Times are changing and facts can be found online or with a calculator, but these educators are ignoring a key word: *foundational.* Students have to know the foundations in order to build on them later. They cannot constantly be looking up basic facts.

As a middle school math teacher, I see firsthand how devastating it is for students not to know their multiplication tables. Yes, they can use a calculator when they just need to know what 26 x 5 is, but these students are paralyzed when they have to apply this knowledge to factor a number or reduce a fraction. They cannot reach the next level if they haven't mastered foundational concepts, and no calculator or search engine can do that for them. Apparently, I'm not the only one who has noticed this phenomenon. The journal *Mathematical Cognition* published a study that found that most mistakes students made while solving complex math problems were actually due to their not having an adequate grasp of the basic math facts.[2]

This concept is also true for basic science, history, and English facts. The basics have to be mastered, which often means drilling and memory work. Elementary teachers, determine to teach and drill these important facts.

Middle school/junior high: Once students learn foundational facts, they can engage in critical thinking. Secondary students need to delve deeper to think through the *why* behind the concepts that they've learned. It's time to move past elementary rote memorization to higher-level thinking. They should know the foundational concepts, and we are now at the point where much of the knowledge they are learning could, in fact, be found using a search engine. We need to teach them to analyze and evaluate information that they find, to take words and draw conclusions from them. Most importantly, we must teach them to filter everything through a biblical worldview.

2. J. Joy Cumming and John Elkins, "Lack of Automaticity in Basic Addition Facts as a Characteristic of Arithmetic Learning Problems and Instructional Needs," *Mathematical Cognition*, 5 (2) (1999), 149-180.

High school: We hope that by the time a student reaches high school, he has already mastered the foundational concepts and is developing the ability to think critically about them. High school classes should not only continue to hone students' critical thinking skills, but they should also teach students how to communicate their knowledge. In our ever-changing society, students must be able to express themselves clearly and concisely. They should learn these skills not just in English class, but across all disciplines. It's not enough for high schoolers just to know facts. They need to be able to analyze them, draw conclusions, and articulate their views. A great way to help students learn to express themselves is through writing to learn. See Appendix B for more information on this topic.

I realize this is idealistic. Secondary teachers will likely have students in their classroom who need extra help because they're behind, but most of your students should be ready to learn. If they're not, go back to the beginning. Don't try to build on a foundation that hasn't already been laid.

Journal: Elementary teachers: How effective have you been at teaching and drilling foundational concepts with your students? Secondary teachers: Do you go beyond the foundations to critical thinking and communication? What do you need to adjust to fulfill these goals in your classroom?

Lesson 24:
The Order of Things

"I don't get it!" We never like to hear these words come out of our students' mouths. Sometimes students don't understand because they're not paying attention, but other times, our lessons are just confusing. While we'll never completely eliminate confusion, our job is to make the material as clear as we possibly can. Mrs. Judy Howe, a veteran teacher and textbook author for A Beka Book, maintains that for skill subjects such as math, grammar, and writing, the best way to teach a new concept is to use the following order:

1. You explain the concept.

2. You practice the concept with the students.

3. The students practice the concept on their own.

Let's say you are teaching your students how to multiply two-digit numbers. First, you should explain the concept to them, using an example and working through each step carefully. You may work one or many examples depending on the difficulty of the concept and how well the students seem to be comprehending the lesson.

Next, practice the concept with the students. This is an extremely important piece of the lesson because now the students should be starting to think through the process with you. Every step of the way, you should be asking questions like, "What do we do next?" "What is 4 times 5?" "What do we need to remember to do with the second row?" Do a few problems (or grammar sentences or writing exercises) together, giving the students less and less help each time.

The last step is for students to practice on their own, but don't leave them on their own. Walk around answering questions, correcting misunderstandings, and guiding confused students. Don't forget to go over the answers so students can see what they did wrong. (Practice questions can come from the book, a worksheet, or the chalkboard.)

You don't have to finish all three steps in one day as long as you follow the pattern. For example, you can teach and practice with the students one day and then have them practice on their own the next.

Journal: Honestly evaluate how well your students understand your explanations. How can you improve their understanding? If necessary, ask another teacher for help.

Lesson 25:
One-on-One

Students learn best through one-on-one, personalized instruction. Unfortunately, this is nearly impossible in a traditional classroom. No teacher can possibly provide individual tutoring for each of his many students. Or can he?

We talked in the last lesson about moving around the room during work times, and I have found this to be an incredible help to my students. One-on-one interaction during work times allows for personalized instruction and tutoring within the traditional classroom.

If you're like me, the biggest obstacle you have to overcome while students are working is fighting the urge to get some grading done. I completely understand this, but I want to encourage you to instead give this time to your students. I think you'll be happy with the results. If you really need to use class work times to complete your own work, at least consider walking around the room periodically.

Once you decide to implement this strategy, you'll need to plan work times into your class schedules. Give students assignments to do on their own – problems to solve, questions to answer, or pieces to write. Make sure the work is valuable and helps the students better understand the material. During these work times, walk around the room and assist students as needed. Sometimes you'll stay busy with raised hands, but other times you'll be able to be more strategic. Focus on the students who are struggling, even if they don't ask for help. You can also stop to read students' work and offer suggestions for improvement. While the main purpose of walking around is helping students, you'll also be able to prevent and correct discipline issues. There's a good chance you wouldn't have noticed that student writing a note if you had stayed at your desk.

I have personally found this approach to work well with math and writing in particular. With both of these skills, students often need pointers and direction.

Journal: How can you incorporate one-on-one help into your classroom? What types of assignments would work well with this strategy?

Lesson 26:
Time Out

As we discussed in Lesson 3, taking time to reflect can help us reorient our priorities and identify areas in which we can improve. If you're in the middle of the whirlwind of teaching, counseling, preparing, and grading, you may find it difficult to step back for a few minutes and reflect. But busyness doesn't make this step any less important. With our study halfway done, today's lesson once again provides an opportunity for reflection.

Try to find time this week to think and pray. If you're in the middle of a busy year, you probably don't have the luxury of blocking off half an hour during the school day. But that doesn't mean you don't have time to reflect. Start by meditating on the following questions for a day or two. Think and pray about them during free moments, commutes home, or during monitoring duties. Then, try to find a few moments to sit down and journal your responses. This could happen during school, but it may work better during an evening or over the weekend.

Before we get to the questions, take a minute to look back at the description of your dream classroom from Lesson 1 and your reflection from Lesson 3. In particular, note the areas you listed as your top three priorities for change.

Then start considering these questions:

1. Have your top priorities been addressed yet? If not, what are some possible solutions?

2. What have you learned? How have you improved your classroom?

3. What areas of your classroom still need improvement?

4. In what areas do you need encouragement or help?

5. What has God been teaching you about your teaching?

6. What advice can you share with other teachers?

Don't forget to bathe this process in prayer. Pray about your strengths and weaknesses, your classroom, and the questions you still have. God cares about every detail of our lives, and He certainly cares about helping you become the best teacher you can so you can fulfill the calling He has given you.

Put it into practice/Journal: After contemplating these questions, take time to journal your responses. Seek other teachers' help for the areas in which you still need advice or encouragement. Share your experience and the lessons you've learned with others as well. You can do this in person and also in online in our Facebook discussion group, Teach 4 the Heart's Christian Teachers' Lounge.

Lesson 27:
When Things Get Crazy

Few people understand the word *busy* better than teachers. There is always so much to do and so little time to do it. And when we do get to our planning times, something else inevitably comes up. A student asks for help, an administrator wants to meet with us, or a parent needs to be called.

At times, the schedule can be overwhelming. And we all react differently. My natural reaction is to put my head down, make a list, get focused, and get it done. But that's not always the best reaction. I may get things crossed off my list, but I'm also likely to walk right by a hurting student without even noticing. I might grade papers while a student is trying to talk to me. My tasks get finished, but my true mission remains unfulfilled.

I understand better than most the temptation to barricade yourself in your room with your red pen and coffee. But if we really want to be effective, we need to keep the big picture in mind.

The following principles, most of which can be found in Stephen Covey's book *The 7 Habits of Highly Effective People,* were first shared with me by my principal Bill Blankschaen. I wish I could say I always remember them, but that's just not the case. It's a work in progress, but it's definitely worth the effort.

1. **Do what is important, not necessarily what's urgent.** When I first heard this phrase, I loved it so much that I laminated it and put it up on the wall right by my desk. What a great reminder that the stack of papers screaming at me can wait, but the student who acted out in class today needs a genuine, unrushed conversation, not just a one-liner and a detention slip.

2. **Slow is fast, and fast is slow.** This principle is one that I have not even begun to master, but the more I contemplate it, the more I see its truth. When it comes to our relationships (which at school include students, parents, administrators, and fellow teachers), rushing through a conversation often backfires. We get to cross the task off our list, but since we didn't take the time to really get to the root of the issue, the problem springs right back up like a weed that hasn't been dug out by the roots. We think we're saving time, but we're really just wasting it. Fast is slow.

   On the other hand, when we take the time to have the in-depth conversation that's really needed, we are much more effective. So if we can learn to turn off the panic alarms in our heads and truly counsel our students, we may actually find real solutions that will make a difference. Slow is fast.

3. **Focus is more valuable than multitasking.** My name is Linda, and I am a chronic multitasker. Yes, I am addicted to it. But I'm trying to learn the value of focus. While

multitasking is sometimes helpful, it often makes us less effective at all the tasks we're trying to do. So if you're trying to accomplish a high-level task such as planning lessons or counseling students, tune out the rest of your to-do list and focus on the task at hand. The list won't go anywhere while you're gone.

Journal: How do you respond to the busyness of teaching? What do you want to do differently? How can you remember these principles during stressful days?

Lesson 28:
And the Participation
Award Goes To...

Don't you love participation awards? I think most kids recognize them for what they are – pieces of paper meant to make them feel better for not winning. However, if schools awarded a participation award to the teacher who had the most students actively participating in class, that would be a valuable award indeed.

Some students can learn simply by watching, but more often than not, if students aren't actively participating, they aren't actively learning. They might be picking up a thing or two between daydreams, but they're definitely not learning all that they could. The more involved students are in the learning process, the more they will remember.

So how can you get your students more involved? Here are a few ideas:

1. **Call on students even when they don't raise their hand.** This is a simple idea, but it's something I have to remind myself to do. Try to call on every student every class period (or every subject for elementary). Don't call on students who struggle for the hard questions; call on them for the easier questions to help build confidence. You can also try putting a student's name at the end of the question instead

of the beginning. Ask, "Who was the first President, Elisha?" instead of "Elisha, who was the first President?" If you put the name first, the rest of the class can tune out right from the start, but if the name always comes at the end, the whole class must pay attention to the question. Better yet, ask the question and then pause to let the entire class think before choosing a student.

2. **Have students complete work in class.** Try to structure your classes so that you are not lecturing the entire time. You've likely heard that we remember only 10 percent of what we hear but 80 percent of what we do. So make sure your students actually *do* something. This is easy in math and English where students can practice problems, grammar, or writing. Other subjects require a little more creativity, but shouldn't pose too much of a problem. History students can put the Bill of Rights in their own words; science students can conduct an experiment.

   Make sure these activities are not just "filler." You're not helping your students by giving them an activity that wastes time. A two-week animal sculpture may be a great art project, but it's a huge waste of time in science class.

3. **Use writing.** When you ask your class to write down an answer, everyone must actively think. So make it a habit to ask students to write. For example, if you want to have a class discussion on a topic, first ask the students to get out a sheet of paper and give them a couple minutes to write down their thoughts. During the discussion, you can then ask the students what they wrote. If you want to take your classroom

to the next level, you can learn more about incorporating writing into your subject by turning to Appendix B and reading *Content-Area Writing: Every Teacher's Guide* by Daniels, Zemelman, and Steineke. We'll also discuss this idea more in Lesson 49.

4. **Use the chalkboard/white board.** Have students present their answers on the board for the class. This works especially well with homework. While the class works on an assignment, have some of the students write answers on the board (for math, make sure they include their work). Each student completes one question. Then, have the students present their problems to the class, explaining how they found the answer. The class can then ask questions, and you have the option of answering them yourself or deferring to the students to answer. We'll discuss this idea in more detail in the next lesson.

5. **Have the entire class answer.** Ask a question and tell everyone to say the answer on the count of three. Not only does this provide variety, but it also gets more students involved without singling out the shy or less confident learners. This also provides a great opportunity for you to quickly gauge how well students are learning. Use this method to drill new concepts or help students memorize. Have the entire class recite multiplication tables, poems, or Bible verses out loud.

Journal: How can you improve your students' participation?

Connect: Share your ideas and suggestions on our discussion page at teach4theheart.com/discussions.

Lesson 29:
Come on Down

"Can I please put up a problem?" "If anyone's absent, can I do theirs?" "I got #5. Can I do it?" My sixth grade math class greets me with a torrent of questions. Although it's slightly overwhelming, I'm encouraged by their enthusiasm. While not all ages respond with this much excitement at the prospect of doing math problems in front of the class, they can all benefit from being called down to the board.

Pensacola Christian Academy uses this method with incredible success. Here's how the teachers do it: Before class starts, the teacher writes on the board the names of the students who will provide the answers. When class starts (or at the appropriate time) those students write their answers on the board while the rest of the class completes an assignment. Once all the answers are up, it's time to review the work. (If you want to grade the assignment, this is the time.)

The beauty of this method is that the teacher does not go over the problems; the students do. One at a time, the students present their answers to the class, explaining their work. The teacher can then take questions before the problems get erased. Sometimes the teacher may answer the questions himself, but often he refers the questions to the students, giving them the opportunity to defend their answers.

By using this system, you're saving time, since the students are writing all the answers at once, rather than one at a time. You're also helping students actively participate in class while you're holding them accountable for their work. Most importantly, you're teaching your students how to speak in public and explain their thought process.

Journal: Would having students write answers on the board work in your classroom? If so, what would it look like?

Lesson 30:
Can We Play a Game?

If your students are anything like mine, the question, "Can we play a game?" is asked about a hundred times a week. I may be exaggerating, but I sure hear it frequently, considering my answer is typically no. I recognize that games can certainly provide a good change of pace for students while keeping them engaged. However, when it's time to review for a test, I am always concerned that we don't waste precious time on a game when we desperately need a thorough review. Fortunately, we can do both. By choosing games that focus on the questions themselves while spending minimal time on the "game" part, we can give our students a change of pace without sacrificing the review.

Here are some games that use time efficiently:

1. **Just give points:** Simply divide the class into two (or more) teams and start asking questions. Call on the first hand raised, and if he's right, give his team a point. If he's wrong, the other teams get a chance to answer. Keep a tally on the board, and the team with the most points at the end wins.

2. **Personal whiteboards:** If you're able to invest a little money, purchase personal-sized whiteboards and dry erase markers, enough for each student. You ask questions, and the students write the answers on their boards and hold them up. The first correct answer wins a point. This game wastes almost no time, and the kids love it. (If you want to save money, you can create your own whiteboards by laminating sheets of cardboard or cardstock. Students would then write with wet-erase markers.)

3. **Race at the board:** Divide the class into two or three teams. One representative from each team comes to the board. You ask a question or give a problem, and the first person to write the correct answer on the board wins a point for his team. The students at the board only get one try, though. If they all miss the question, you take the answer from the first person in the audience who raises his hand. Just be sure to keep this game moving to minimize wasted time from students moving to and from the board.

4. **Group work:** Assign a set of questions or problems to be answered by the group in a set amount of time. The group with the most correct wins. You're really just adding a contest to a regular assignment, but the students appreciate the twist, especially if it comes with a prize such as a bonus point, homework pass, or candy.

5. **Football**: Draw a "football field" on your board like the one seen here. Create a football magnet and place it at one end. Divide the class into two teams. Ask a question to the first team. If they get it right, move the football one line towards

their end zone and ask another question. If they miss it, that's a turnover, and the other team starts getting questions. The football then moves toward their end with every correct response. Whenever a team gets the football into their end zone, they score a touchdown.

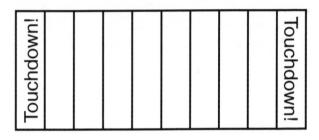

6. **Un-Wheel of Fortune:** This is Wheel of Fortune without the wheel. Have a phrase for the students to solve (preferably a key term or concept you are studying). Divide the class into two teams and ask questions to each student, going back and forth between the teams. Tally points for each team as follows: If the student answers correctly, give one point and allow him to choose a letter. Award additional points for each time the letter appears. (For example, if Gavin guesses *E* and there are 3 *E*'s, he gets 4 points: 1 for the correct answer and 3 for the 3 *E*'s.) The student can then try to guess the puzzle. Award 5 points to the team that solves the puzzle.

7. **Around the World**: This classic individual game still works so well! The first two students pair off against each other. You ask a question, and whoever says the answer first wins. The winner stands up and moves to the next contestant. The goal is to move as many seats as possible before losing, at

which point the losing student sits in the seat of the person who beat him. The game ideally continues until one student makes it "around the world" and gets all the way back to his own seat. Often, though, the game simply ends when time is up, and the person who travelled the farthest wins.

Connect: What games do you use in your classroom? Share them on our discussion page at teach4theheart.com/discussions.

Lesson 31:
Prayer Focus: Wisdom

In James 1:5, Scripture teaches that if anyone lacks wisdom, he should ask God, who gives to all generously and without reproach, and God will give it to him. What a precious promise for us as teachers! Every day we face situations that, if handled on our own, will end very poorly. Yet God promises to give us His wisdom if we just ask. And better yet, He promises to give generously and without reproaching us for asking.

We need to pray for wisdom both intentionally and spontaneously. We should make a specific point to entreat God for wisdom every day, and we should also be ready to come before His throne when a specific situation arises for which we need His guidance. Then we must listen for His response.

Today we are setting aside time to pray for wisdom, but before we do, I would like to provide a few pieces of practical advice in this regard:

1. **Wisdom is found in God's Word.** The better we know the Bible, the more God will be able to bring verses to our mind in response to prayers for wisdom. That's why it's so important to spend time in God's Word daily to allow Him to speak to us and show us His truths.

2. **Press pause.** When you don't immediately know how to handle a situation, wait. Tell the student that you will speak with him later in the day. Give God time to answer your prayer and provide you with clarity and direction. We all know that it's not smart to put off dealing with problems, but giving yourself time to think and hear from God is a worthwhile reason to wait.

3. **Ask advice.** Proverbs 11:14 states, "In the multitude of counselors there is safety." God often speaks to us through the advice of others. If you have fellow teachers who are wise and godly, seek their advice whenever a difficult question arises.

Put it into practice: Spend time in prayer asking God for wisdom. Be specific about the areas in which you most need help. Listen for God's response.

Connect: Share your prayer requests in Teach 4 the Heart's Christian Teachers' Lounge, our Facebook discussion group.

Lesson 32:
Stick with the Green Pen

I ask my students to bring a green pen to class every day to use in grading each other's homework. Since they do their math in pencil, they use green to grade so that I know no one is writing in answers for a friend. Most students faithfully bring their green pens, but I find that there are always a few who are missing theirs and trying to discreetly substitute black or blue. After fighting this trend for a year or two, I had a revelation one summer – why not just require any pen instead of green? I figured everyone should always have a pen, students still wouldn't be able to change answers, and I'd eliminate the headache of insisting on green. A good plan? I thought so, but it wasn't. The next year most of the students had a pen, but the same students who used to sneak a blue or black pen instead of green now had no pen at all. My problem had not been solved; instead, it had grown worse.

The issue wasn't that I had an unreasonable expectation, but that I was fighting human nature. There will always be students who test the boundaries. Always. So when I lowered the bar to try to accommodate those students, they lowered their effort as well. While this is a relatively unimportant example, I have found this principle to be fairly consistent across the board. If you lower your standard because you think some students won't meet your high expectations, most students lower their effort to align with the lower standard. And you end up dealing with bigger problems later on.

As a teacher, you'll deal with student issues no matter what. The question is whether those issues will be big or small. If you expect your students to pay attention, work hard, and stay on task, you will find that most of the problems you deal with will be small. However, if your expectation is simply that the kids aren't fighting with each other, then you will have to deal with fist fights. You'll always have students who push the boundaries; you just get to decide if they cross the line into small problems or big ones.

Please don't misunderstand and decide to set unreasonable standards. These are incredibly frustrating to the majority of the class who are good students trying to meet your expectations. Instead, define reasonable, appropriate expectations and determine not to lower these standards just to avoid confrontation with disruptive students.

What expectations do you need to raise in your class? What's your green pen?

Journal: Carefully think about your expectations for your classroom. What expectations need to be established or improved? Below are some areas you may want to consider:

1. Talking/communication
2. Homework
3. Tardiness
4. Restroom

5. Kindness

6. Respect

7. Participation

8. Moving around the classroom

9. Effort

Put it into practice (summer): Make a list of behaviors you will expect of your students next year. (Please note that you're not creating a list of rules that you will hand out to your students. It's a list for *you* so that you know what types of behavior you will verbally correct.)

Put it into practice (school year): If you've started to let your standards slip, it's time to have a talk with your students and reestablish them. Decide which expectations you should raise now and which you should wait to change until next year. Generally, low standards that are causing problems in your class should be changed now, even though the process may be challenging. Start by telling the students what you expect of them. Then patiently and consistently remind them when they fall short. Determine consequences for repeat offenders.

Lesson 33:
An Ounce of Prevention

The students have finished their quiz and exchanged their papers. The teacher then reads the answers so the class can grade each other's' quizzes. But the students aren't grading. What the teacher fails to notice is that the students actually just exchanged blank sheets of paper and are writing in the correct answers for each other as he reads them. An outrageous example? Actually, no. My husband admits that his classmates did this all the time in one of his high school classes.

We're spending lots of time discussing how to deal with discipline problems, but we can also prevent a lot of issues from happening in the first place. Solid procedures may never completely eliminating problems, but they can certainly minimize them. Our procedures should help students make the right choices while making it as difficult as possible for them to do wrong. As seen in our example, if we make cheating easy, our students will quickly fall to the temptation. Conversely, if cheating takes much more work than honesty, they may not even be tempted in the first place. Below are some examples of procedures that help prevent problems:

1. **Don't allow students to grade their own papers if you are counting them as a grade**. It's too tempting for students to be dishonest when they grade their own work. I only allow students to correct their own papers if I'm not taking the assignment for a grade.

2. **Have students grade using a different color, and have them remove other writing utensils from their desks**. In my math classroom where students take quizzes in pencil, they are required to grade in pen. All pencils have to be off their desks. Although I hope you wouldn't be as oblivious as the teacher in our example, it's just too easy for students to make minor changes to their friend's paper if they're using the same instrument.

3. **Have students use cover sheets when taking tests or quizzes**. This is just a blank sheet of paper that students use to cover their answers as they take tests or quizzes. Answers that are just sitting out in the open are too tempting for some students. Without cover sheets, even students who don't want to cheat could see an answer and face a moral dilemma. Help prevent this whole mess by requiring your students to use cover sheets.

4. **Have students clear their desks**. Train your students to only have on their desks what they need and put away books for other classes. This allows you to see exactly what they are doing. Students can easily write notes or work on homework for another class when they have a huge pile of books to hide behind. It's not so easy when the only thing they have on

their desks is the assignment they're working on. You will probably have to remind your students to clear their desks over and over before it becomes habit, but the extra effort up front will be worthwhile.

5. **Use assigned seats and change them periodically.** Once you know your students, you can assign seats strategically – separating chatty friends and placing struggling students near the front. Once you set new seats, don't hesitate to tweak the arrangement, switching a few students whenever you notice a problem.

6. **Use monitors.** Elementary teachers may want to assign a student monitor who is responsible for the classroom when you step out of the room or during bathroom breaks.

Journal: Think through the areas of your classroom that were difficult last year and brainstorm procedures you can put in place to prevent some of those issues.

Lesson 34:
More Than a Punishment

Classroom discipline often deals with the little things – talking in class, being tardy, or lacking the right supplies. Other times, however, the stakes are much higher, and we are dealing with issues of character and integrity. In these cases, we must speak to the heart, rather than simply handing out punishments. We must engage the students on a spiritual level and speak God's truth to them.

Entire books have been written on this one topic, and I can't do it justice in a few short paragraphs. However, I would like to share with you a few thoughts I learned from watching my principal Bill Blankschaen counsel and discipline students:

1. **Speak to the heart.** If we don't address the heart, we won't accomplish anything of lasting value. We may be able to threaten or force students to obey our rules while they're sitting in our classroom, but if that's all we do, we're missing the big picture. Our goal is not just to educate students, but also to disciple them and to instill character in them. The only way to do this is to get to the heart of the issue and speak God's truth to their spirit.

2. Use Scripture. God's Word is alive and powerful and never returns void. Use His truth as you speak to students. If you need to, prepare a list of Scriptures that address common discipline situations you may face. If you teach in a public school, you should still use Scripture; just rephrase it. Instead of saying, "The Bible says, 'Be kind one to another,'" say something like, "We must be kind and forgiving to each other." God's Word is still powerful, even if you can't tell them it's from the Bible.

3. Ask questions. When we do all the talking, students believe they're getting a lecture and tune us out until we're done. If, however, you ask the student a question, you force him to engage in the conversation. You also gain valuable insight into his thinking. Let his answers guide the direction of the conversation. And if he doesn't answer immediately, don't be afraid to wait silently until he does.

4. Be calm and kind. Remember that a student's heart can only be changed if he's able to focus on the truth being spoken and not get distracted by a teacher's demeaning attitude.

5. Pray for wisdom. In James 1:5, God promises to give us wisdom if we ask Him for it. Pray daily for God's guidance, and, if possible, pray with your student as you start your conversation. Ask God to give you His wisdom and guide your words.

6. Learn from others. Ask a mentor teacher or your principal if you would be able to sit in on some conversations with students. There is no substitute for seeing biblical discipleship modeled in front of you. I had the privilege to observe my principal speak with students a few times, and I learned so much from these opportunities.

Journal: As teachers, we have an incredible opportunity to speak to our students' hearts. Write down your thoughts and prayers in this area.

Put it into practice: Make a list of Scriptures that deal with various topics that may come up. (I could just give you a list, but half the value is in finding them yourself, becoming familiar with them, and letting them speak to you.) Topics may include anger, cheating, lying, gossiping, unkindness, disrespect, disobedience, sexual purity and taking the Lord's name in vain.

Connect: In this most important area of teaching, we need to learn from each other. Share your wisdom or ask questions on our discipline discussion page at teach4theheart.com/discussions.

To study this topic in more detail, read *Shepherding a Child's Heart* by Tedd Tripp.

Lesson 35:
More Than Sentences

I I I I I I I I I will will will will will will will not not not not not not
not...

Have you seen students working on these sentences? Maybe you
remember completing some yourself, or maybe you've given them
out. We all realize sentences are not the most effective means of
discipline, but we sometimes assign them because we can't think of
a better alternative. I would like to suggest something a little better
than sentences.

Before we get to that, we need to discuss when you might need an
alternative discipline option. Every school's discipline structure is
set up differently, and some teachers have smaller measures available
to them such as lunch detentions or demerits. Other schools do not
have as many options. In my school, detentions are two hours long
and cost the family $20. This works well as a solid punishment but
is too much, in my opinion, to address smaller classroom issues. The
problem I run into is that if I wait to give out any punishment until
a detention is warranted, I end up letting way too much go (like we
talked about in Lesson 5). I need some smaller punishments.

If your situation is similar to mine, discipline essays may be the way to go. The first type of discipline essay is similar to sentences, except the student must copy a paragraph or two that discuss their behavior, the reason it was wrong, what is appropriate, and the applicable biblical principles. At least you're reinforcing the lesson you are trying to teach instead of just making the student write the same words over and over. (Students also typically prefer short sentences over these long paragraphs, making the essays a more effective deterrent).

The second option is for the student to write his own essay from guided questions that you have prepared. This engages students more as they must actually think about what to write as opposed to simply copying words. Make sure you give requirements for how long each answer must be.

One other piece of advice: require a parent's signature. This will often make a huge difference in how the student perceives the discipline and may even be a better deterrent than the assignment itself.

For either method, you can have essays prepped ahead of time for common problems such as talking, distracting others, not participating in class, and being unkind. Have them written out with instructions on the top so that all you have to do is grab one from a folder and hand it to the student. If they're ready to go, you'll be more likely to use them. See Appendix C for examples of both types of essays.

Put it into practice: If you think this method may work for you, prepare essays for some of your most common problems. You can start with the examples in Appendix C and adapt them to fit your classroom.

Lesson 36:
The Power of Quiet

"That's it!" screams the irate teacher, a vein in his forehead popping out as he hurls a piece of chalk at the offending student. "I've had it with you!"

Unfortunately, I witnessed such scenes a few times when I was in school, and they were never pretty. The irony is that when a situation like this arises, the teacher's response becomes a punch line. The story becomes legend among students, and respect for the teacher gets chipped away with each retelling. Normally, students do not learn their lesson in these situations. Laughing at the teacher's reaction serves as an alternative to honestly examining their own actions.

Should students react this way? Of course not. But they do. And because they do, we need to realize that yelling at students in anger does more harm than good.

Handle every student discipline issue calmly and in love. When we take the time to speak to a student after class in a quiet (but firm) voice, explaining what he did wrong and what the punishment will be, we are much more effective. Without distracting theatrics, both teacher and student are free to discuss the issue at hand. We also demonstrate to the student how to handle difficult situations effectively.

I can't overstate the power of quiet. The next time a student disrupts class, try this: instead of yelling, walk to that student's desk, stop teaching, and whisper a correction to him. This will be just as effective, and the whole class will notice and likely straighten up. Or, just stop teaching and stare at the offending student until he notices. You may not even have to say a word. He'll get the message.

One of the most powerful examples of this I have ever witnessed took place during one of my college speech lectures. A young graduate assistant was lecturing about 150 underclassmen and, for some reason, everyone in the class started talking. The teacher had clearly lost control of the class, and I (as an education student) watched with interest to see how she would respond. She didn't yell or scream. Instead, she just stopped teaching and waited in silence. Soon the class realized what was happening and quieted down, and I will never forget what she said next. In a firm but calm voice she just said, "I *will* have your attention." My jaw dropped in amazement as an entire room of unruly students sat up straight and did just that – gave her their full attention. She continued with her lesson, having just earned the respect of the class.

Learning to deal with discipline calmly is more difficult for some than others. If you become angry easily, ask God for help. Memorize Scripture that you can remember in the heat of the moment such as Proverbs 15:18, which states, "A wrathful man stirreth up strife, but he that is slow to anger appeaseth strife." As you pray and seek to deal with situations correctly, you will find yourself building good habits. However, as you grow, you may still fall into anger. Don't be discouraged. God forgives and so will your students if you're humble enough to ask their forgiveness. Asking students' forgiveness for flying off the handle can be extremely powerful, because it shows them that you respect them and can admit when you are wrong. During these times, you have the powerful opportunity to teach by example.

If you've found yourself reacting in anger to your students, spend time in prayer, then seek wisdom from a teacher who seems to have this issue under control. Ask him to be your prayer partner in this area and to help keep you accountable. For more insight, read *Your Reactions Are Showing* by J. Allan Petersen.

Journal: How do you handle discipline situations? Do you typically react in anger or are you able to keep your cool? What helps you? What do you need to change?

Lesson 37:
Everyone Loves Rewards

Has anyone not loved receiving a reward? They make us feel proud of our accomplishment and appreciated by the giver. Of course, we also get to enjoy the benefits of the reward itself. Talk about a pick-me-up! Getting a reward, or even just an appreciative word, can often make all the difference.

Considering the encouraging power of rewards, why would we withhold them our students? While we need to be cautious of conditioning our students to expect and demand rewards (leading to an entitlement mentality), we also need to remember that God rewards us. He is our model in all things, so if He rewards righteousness, I think we should too. Let's look at a few Scriptures about God's rewards:

> Ephesians 6:2-3: Honor your father and mother, which is the first commandment with promise: that it may be well with you and you may live long on the earth.

> Psalm 18:20: The Lord rewarded me according to my righteousness; According to the cleanness of my hands He has recompensed me.

Matthew 6:3-4: But when you do a charitable deed, do not let your left hand know what your right hand is doing, that your charitable deed may be in secret; and your Father who sees in secret will Himself reward you openly

Matthew 6:6: But you, when you pray, go into your room, and when you have shut your door, pray to your Father who is in the secret place; and your Father who sees in secret will reward you openly.

Matthew 6:17-18: But you, when you fast, anoint your head and wash your face, so that you do not appear to men to be fasting, but to your Father who is in the secret place; and your Father who sees in secret will reward you openly.

Sometimes we don't give rewards because of the time and money involved. Fortunately, rewards don't require a lot of time; they just require some planning. Put reminders in your calendar if you need to. You can also give rewards that cost little to no money. The rewards listed below show appreciation while costing you almost nothing:

1. **A kind word/note** – Simply telling a student you appreciate his work or behavior can be more powerful than you realize. Better yet, write your appreciation in a note. Or, email his parents telling them how proud you are of their child.

2. **Homework passes** – All this takes is printing up a sheet of paper saying the student is exempt from homework.

3. **Skip the odds pass** – This is similar to a homework pass except that a student gets to skip all of the odd-numbered questions/problems, essentially cutting his homework in half. This is great because it still allows the student to practice the lesson.

4. **Free seating days/classes** – Students love this one. I love it too because it is free and easy. I have a board in my classroom and award a check to the class whenever they do something good. When they earn ten checks, they earn a free seating day. The only downside is that students tend to be a little less focused when they sit with their friends. But it's worth it.

5. **Having class outside** – If possible, conduct class outside in nice weather as a reward. Better yet, plan a learning activity that can occur outside.

6. **Candy** – This one obviously costs a little bit, but you can buy big bags of candy so that each individual piece is very cheap.

7. **Dress-down day** – This idea needs administrative approval, but consider dress-down days for major prizes. Just be sure to specify what is appropriate on a dress-down day.

8. **Extra recess**– Who doesn't love a little more free time?

9. **Bonus points** – I still don't understand why students go crazy for bonus points, but they do. Just make sure you don't award too many bonus points so that their grades become inaccurate.

Note that some of the rewards are for the whole class, while others are individual. It's great to have a mix of both. This list is by no means exhaustive, but I hope it's getting your brain rolling with creative ideas for student rewards.

Journal: How do you reward your students? How can you improve in this area? Be creative.

Connect: We'd love to hear your ideas on our discussion page at teach4theheart.com/discussions.

Lesson 38:
The Case for Mercy

Let's say you teach a student who has really been struggling in his behavior, academics, and attitude. Halfway through the year the principal decides that if the student gets another detention for the rest of the year, he will be expelled. As you watch this student over the next two months, you are thrilled to see genuine change in his behavior. He is making a real effort and has shown incredible improvement. Best of all, the outward change appears to be a result of genuine heart repentance. One Friday, the bell rings and he comes sprinting into your classroom – late again. It's his second time this quarter, and according to your policy, he should receive a detention. But that would likely result in his expulsion. What should you do?

One of the most difficult questions in Christian discipline is how to balance consequences and mercy. I can't give you a correct response for this scenario. You'll need to consider multiple factors and pray for wisdom from God. However, I can tell you that there are times when mercy is appropriate. Discipling the hearts of your students is much more important than slavishly following every line of your discipline code in order to be fair. We shouldn't deviate from our normal course of action all the time, but we should be sensitive to the Holy Spirit's leading in these areas. We sure are glad when God gives us mercy, and there are times when it is appropriate to do so with our students.

If you do feel led to give mercy, you should typically still speak with the student (instead of just pretending that you didn't notice). Explain to him that you are being very merciful this time but if he is late again, there will be no more mercy left, and he will receive a detention. Ideally, the student will heed the warning and not be late again, in which case you will have a thankful, on-time student the rest of the year. If he's tardy again, you can give the detention, knowing that the student understands that he's been given extra mercy. Either way, you've shown compassion while achieving your desired outcome.

If you're concerned that this isn't fair, I would submit to you that God is not fair. And we sure are glad He's not. He is just, but if He were fair, none of us would ever have anything good because, frankly, we don't deserve it. If God were fair, we would all be punished every time we messed up. In fact, we would all be burning in hell right now. That's fair.

Furthermore, God is not fair in His blessings either; He gives as He deems best. If you don't believe me, read the parable of the workers in Matthew 20:1-16. If He were fair, we certainly wouldn't live in America with all of our blessings while others wallow in poverty in Africa or are persecuted for their faith in Pakistan. God is always good to us, but He doesn't treat us all the same. He treats each of us as individuals and works in each life uniquely as He sees fit to grow us according to His plan.

While you should never play favorites in your classroom, keep this truth in mind during those situations when you feel led to deal with a student uniquely. If you are worried about the other students' reaction, speak with them about God's fairness. It's always an interesting conversation. When you first ask them if they want life to be fair, they say yes, yes, yes! But then when you start explaining what that would look like, they soon realize how blessed they are. None of us want life to truly be fair. Helping your students understand this truth is much more powerful than just throwing out the cliché, "Life's not fair."

The answers are never simple, but when God started showing me His truths about fairness, I really started thinking. I hope today's thoughts will encourage you to dive deeper into His Word and think through these areas for yourself. In the next lesson we'll deal with the danger on the other end of the spectrum – too much mercy.

Journal: What is God teaching you about mercy in your classroom?

Connect: The more we discuss this topic, the more we learn and grow. Share your thoughts on our discipline discussion page at teach4theheart.com/discussions.

Lesson 39:
First Came the Law

Yesterday, we talked about why mercy is important. However, there's also the danger of giving too much mercy, or maybe more accurately, giving mercy in the wrong way or at the wrong time. This is an area in which I am still learning myself, but God has been showing me a truth that I'd like to share with you – that the law came before mercy.

In dealing with His chosen people, the Israelites, God first gave the law. Then grace and mercy came centuries later at the cross. I believe this was intentional and has applications for our classrooms today. Romans 3:20 states that "by the law is the knowledge of sin" and Galatians 3:24 further explains that "the law was our schoolmaster to bring us unto Christ, that we might be justified by faith." The law had to come first so that man would understand sin and its punishment. Without the law, we wouldn't appreciate grace when Christ offered it because we wouldn't know how lost we were without Him. In giving the law first, God confronted us with our sin and its consequences, so when grace came, we were all amazed at His goodness.

We need to follow this model in our own classrooms. Our students need to understand the law of our classrooms before they can appreciate our mercy. A classroom that starts out by letting everything go in the name of grace will run into difficulty when it inevitably comes time to lay down the law. Students will become confused and resentful when they're being punished for infractions that were winked at earlier in the year. On the other hand, if you start out by kindly but firmly enforcing your rules, your students will appreciate mercy when you choose to give it.

Mercy is incredibly powerful and important, but we must be careful to use it because it is right for the situation, not as an excuse for us to avoid confronting a problem. Being honest with ourselves and open to the leading of the Spirit is key.

Journal: What are some dangers that can occur in giving too much mercy? How can you avoid these?

Lesson 40:
Little White Lies

Adam and Rylie are about to square off in a game of Around the World, the highlight of their week. I flip the flashcard, and the students shout their answers. "Fifty-six!" yells Rylie. "Fifty-eight!" cries Adam. The answers are simultaneous and jumbled, so I ask Adam to repeat his answer. "I said fifty-six," he replies.

A white lie, you may say, but a lie nonetheless. And a lie over a silly game of Around the World. As a teacher, I have seen students lie about nearly every situation imaginable. Lying to get out of trouble, lying about why their homework is missing, lying to win a game, and much more. I'm sure you've seen it too.

It's easy to just gloss over these lies, and I've done my share of glossing. But I'd like to challenge all of us to address these lies for what they are – sin. Our God is a God of truth, and He hates lies. Let's think about a few Scriptures that discuss lying.

> Prov. 12:22: Lying lips are an abomination to the Lord, But those who deal truthfully are His delight.

> Col. 3:9: Do not lie to one another, since you have put off the old man with his deeds.

Prov. 12:19: The lip of truth shall be established forever: but a lying tongue is but for a moment.

Eph. 4:25: Wherefore putting away lying, speak every man truth with his neighbor, for we are members one of another.

God holds truth in high regard, and we should too. We have the opportunity and responsibility to teach students to speak truthfully, so let's take up the challenge and address every lie that we hear this year. Ask the student why he told the lie and listen carefully to his response. (Remember Covey's habit: Seek first to understand then to be understood.) Use Scripture to address the underlying issues behind the lie as well as the lie itself. Sometimes students don't realize that what they're doing is wrong. Yes, they may know that the Bible says not to lie, but they may be so used to it that they don't think it's a big deal. Kindly show them that God places great value on honesty and that they can learn to honor God by being truthful.

By the way, I'm not saying that you should start inquisitions into every statement that could possibly be untrue. You don't have time for these gray hills, and your students will become resentful if you distrust everything that they say. Instead, focus on addressing the situations in which you are faced with a clear lie. You will have plenty of them, I am sure.

Journal: What situations have you encountered in which a student lied to you or others? How will you handle similar situations that arise?

Lesson 41:
But, Why, and How Come?

"But I wasn't talking!" "Why do we have to take notes?" "How come I got in trouble but Casey didn't?" If your students are anything like mine, you hear these questions all too often. These questions and complaints can be annoying at best and intimidating at worst, but handled correctly, they can become great opportunities to disciple students.

As a rookie teacher, I made the mistake of entertaining way too many complaints. I thought that I was being sympathetic by listening to my students when, in reality, the way I handled complaints undermined my own authority. Maybe you are wiser than I, or maybe you've found yourself falling into the same traps. Here are a few lessons I learned the hard way:

1. **Don't respond with anger or argument.** If a student is angry or complaining about a situation, the worst thing we can do is to become angry or argumentative in return. Proverbs 15:1 says that a soft answer turns away wrath. When we give a calm yet firm response to our students, we help diffuse the situation and are much more likely to produce lasting change. If additional consequences are warranted, give them calmly. This will be much more effective than yelling at students and will model Christian character.

2. **Be confident in your authority** and realize that you do not owe the students an explanation. If you believe an explanation will be helpful, then by all means, give one; but if you think the student is merely complaining or testing your authority, you can simply tell him that you don't need to explain yourself. A principle to keep in mind here is that the younger the students, the less explanation they need. You don't have to explain your reasons to a first grader at all, but a senior in high school may benefit from hearing the thought process behind your decision.

3. **Use the magic phrase "because you chose to break the rule."** This phrase is another gem from *The First Days of School*. In my classroom, the rule is no communication without permission. Sometimes when I correct a student, he will respond with an excuse such as, "But I was just asking for a pencil. Why am I in trouble?" To which I answer something like, "I understand, but the rule is no communication, and you chose to break the rule. You should've asked for a pencil before class or raised your hand to say you needed one." Seek to respond with a simple answer that quickly and effectively debunks the excuse.

4. **Be consistent.** The more consistent you are in your response and the less you accept complaints and excuses, the fewer you will get. Teach your students that they may make an appropriate appeal if they have a genuine concern, but complaints and back talking are simply not permitted.

5. **Ask God for wisdom.** We need wisdom to discern between genuine concerns and unnecessary complaints. In our effort to curb complaints and back talk, we must be careful not to shut off all avenues of student appeal. Since we teachers

make mistakes, students need to know that they can come to us with genuine concerns and that we will listen with respect. Ask God to give you wisdom to know when to hear an appeal and when to shut down a complaint.

6. **Seek first to understand**. If a student appears to have a genuine concern, listen carefully to his appeal before you respond. Put yourself in his shoes and honestly consider his request. Few things are more frustrating to a student than when he feels that he has been treated unfairly by his teacher. (Remember how you felt as a student?) If you find you've made a mistake, make it right, and you will gain his respect. If, however, you must deny his request, take the time to speak with him respectfully and disciple him through the process. (See Lesson 8 for reminders about seeking first to understand then to be understood.)

These thoughts only scratch the surface of this complex issue. If you have more questions, seek advice from a wise teacher or ask your questions in Christian Teachers' Lounge.

Journal: How do you handle complaints, excuses, and back talking? Is your approach effective? Why or why not? What do you need to do differently?

Lesson 42:
Confidence

"With confidence, you have won before you have started." This quote by Marcus Garvey epitomizes the difference between my chaotic first-year classroom and my well-established, efficient third-year classroom. I knew what I was supposed to do all along, but during my first months as a teacher, I had no confidence in my ability to discipline. At first, I was scared just to tell a student to sit up. And oh the horror of giving out that first detention! I tried to avoid it as long as possible, and when I finally had to, I was so nervous that I called my husband to help me get up the nerve to approach the student.

The problem is that students can sense fear. It's intangible and unspoken, but a lack of confidence screams to the students that they can try to get away with anything they want. To make matters worse, my lack of confidence kept me from properly dealing with the problems because I didn't feel like I knew what to do. This led to more issues, which I didn't feel comfortable dealing with, which in turn led to bigger problems, which...Well, you get the picture. A few months into the year, I realized that my lack of confidence was a major problem and started dealing with issues. But as you know, reining a class back in once they are already out of control is incredibly difficult, especially since I still lacked – what was it? Oh yeah, confidence.

After several years of teaching, I began to feel comfortable in my role. Because I now know that I can handle any discipline problem that comes up, I exude confidence to my students. When a small problem arises, I handle it. If a big problem arises, I handle it. I may not know ahead of time how I will deal with each situation, but I know that I will take care of it, even if it's by telling the student I will speak with him later in the day (to give myself time to think). Once again, the attitude is intangible and unspoken, but it announces to the students that they need to be on task because misbehavior will not be tolerated.

How did I gain this confidence? By dealing with situations, by finding out that I *could* discipline students, by learning what to say and how to say it. By experience. And that is the difficult part. Confidence is so important, but it's hard to gain if you don't already have it. Faking it won't work for long.

So what should you do if you lack confidence? My best advice is to start building your confidence by role-playing situations that will show up in your classroom. For example, imagine that a student falls asleep during class. Plan exactly what you will say; even writing it out if necessary. Then, practice your response in front of a mirror. Take it a step further by asking a family member or friend to play the student. Do this with as many scenarios as you can imagine, and you should find yourself slowly gaining confidence in your ability to control your classroom.

Journal: How does your confidence (or lack thereof) affect your classroom?

Put it into practice: If you need to develop confidence, start practicing your responses to various scenarios. I've included a list of common issues to get you thinking, but you should start by focusing on the issues you most commonly face. Next time you need to correct a student, respond confidently with your practiced response.

1. Talking without permission

2. Gum chewing

3. Back-talking

4. Tardiness

5. Sleeping in class

6. Late homework

7. Dress code violations

8. Lack of proper supplies

9. Disobedience

10. Not participating in class

11. Lack of effort

12. Swearing

13. Cheating

14. Lying

15. Being unkind to another student

16. Silliness during class

17. Littering

Lesson 43:
Bounced Checks

Imagine this scenario: A student in your class was disruptive today, and now you must speak with him. But you just spoke with him yesterday about not doing his homework and the day before about being unkind to a classmate. In fact, you find yourself always having to get on him for one thing or the other. You sigh and brace yourself for the upcoming confrontation, wondering what on earth you're going to do with this kid.

We've all dealt with similar situations, and we've seen how unhelpful these conversations usually are. After a few incidents, the student is normally not responding well to us or our correction. They're tired of it, we're tired of it, and we're just not making any progress. The reason? The student's emotional bank account is seriously overdrawn, and our checks are bouncing.

Stephen Covey's powerful metaphor of emotional bank accounts, discussed in *The 7 Habits of Highly Effective People*, applies perfectly to the teacher/student relationship. Each student has a bank account into which the teacher can make deposits by showing the student that he cares about him. Then, when a situation arises in which the teacher must confront the student, he can draw on the relationship he has already established. He essentially makes a withdrawal from that student's emotional bank account. The more withdrawals a teacher must make, the more he needs to deposit back into the student's account in order to avoid an overdraft.

Obviously, you must deal with discipline problems when they occur, whether or not you've built a good relationship with the student. But you will be much more effective when you've invested time into the student's life. There are many ways to make deposits into students' emotional bank accounts; here are a few ideas to get you thinking:

1. **Compliment students.** Offer a kind word about anything and everything – good work in class, good behavior, a nice outfit (when appropriate), or a student's performance at a sporting event or drama production.

2. **Write students (or parents) a note.** As a middle school teacher, I normally have about 100 students, but one year I attempted to write each student a personal encouraging note over the course of the year. I then sent a corresponding email to that student's parents with a few kind words. It didn't actually take all that much time, and it was very rewarding.

3. **Show interest in your students' lives.** Try to attend sporting events and activities, remember their birthdays, and ask about their hobbies, families, and interests.

4. **Prioritize.** Put extra thought and prayer into how you can build relationships with your most challenging students.

Journal: How can you be more effective at building relationships with your students?

Connect: We'd love to hear your stories of the difference you saw in a student after you invested time into a relationship. Share them in our Facebook discussion group, Christian Teachers' Lounge.

Lesson 44:
Prayer Focus: Students

If you've taught for any length of time, you've seen all kinds of issues, from those that frustrate you to no end to those that break your heart. We try to handle these problems as best we can, but sometimes we forget our most powerful tool: prayer.

Praying for our students not only provides intercession on their behalf, but also softens our hearts and helps us see them the way God does. We should pray for all of our students, but especially for those for whom we feel particularly burdened or with whom we are experiencing the most difficulty.

Yet we still often forget to pray. Or at least I do. If we're going to pray for our students, we need to be intentional about it. Try putting some reminders in your to-do lists and calendars. Maybe you can develop a system where you pray for particular students on particular days. Or you may want to have a specific time designated for prayer – maybe while you're monitoring students as they take a quiz. Being intentional about scheduling prayer helps us remember what is important because it's just too easy to forget in the rush of busy days.

As you pray for your students, pray in faith, believing that God will work in their lives. I love Andrew Murray's statement, "God means prayer to have an answer, and that it hath not entered into the heart of man to conceive what God will do for His child who gives himself to believe that his prayer will be heard. God hears prayer; this is a truth universally admitted, but of which very few understand the meaning, or experience the power." What a powerful reminder that God has already promised to work if we just ask!

Put it into practice/Journal: Today is one of those intentional moments. Take time right now to pray for your students. Discuss with God your hopes and fears, your joys and challenges.

> **Summer:** Pray that God would lead the right students to your classroom and that He would use you to work in their lives. If you are going to have some of the same students you did last year or if you already have a class roster, pray for them by name.

> **School Year:** Pray for all your students, but pray specifically for those who have great needs. And pray especially for the ones who challenge you.

Connect: Share your prayer requests online in our Christian Teachers' Lounge.

Lesson 45:
Why We Teach

Why are you a teacher? While this can definitely be a question we ask ourselves in exasperation during our most frustrating days, it is a very important question to know the answer to. Your mission and drive will keep you going during those periods when you are overwhelmed or discouraged. If you're not sure that you're doing this because it's what God has for you, you'll find it nearly impossible to make it through difficult days. So take a minute and think about it. Why do you teach?

I teach because I know God has called me to be a teacher. He has given me a passion to not only teach math, but also to help disciple students to be effective servants and leaders for Christ. I am passionate about teaching because, as Henry Adams said, "A teacher affects eternity; he can never tell where his influence stops."

That's my calling. It's simple but powerful because I truly believe God has called me to this work. What's your reason? Whether you've thought for hours about your calling or haven't considered it at all, you will benefit from pausing and taking time to reassess. Think about the calling God has given you and what a privilege it is. Spend time in prayer and Bible reading, thanking God for His guidance and asking Him to continue to lead you. Pray about your mission for this school year.

Perhaps you never envisioned yourself as a teacher but have found yourself in the classroom for one reason or another. You may not even be sure why you're teaching. If you are a teacher just because it's an available job, you probably feel miserable. Therefore, I would challenge you to set aside time for serious prayer. Ask God to clearly show you His calling for you as a teacher, or if you should even be one at all. Maybe He has you in the classroom for a brief time to make you more effective in future ministry. Maybe this will become a life-long journey. Or, possibly, He has a different path for you. You'll either emerge with a clear vision for your time as a teacher or you will realize that God is leading you elsewhere. Either way, you will be drawn closer to God and His plan for your life.

Journal: Why are you a teacher? This can be as short as a sentence or as long as a book, but get something down on paper. Have it available to read during the tough days. It will serve as a valuable reminder and encouragement.

Lesson 46:
Sleeping in the Closet

Tired. That's definitely the word to describe how I feel pretty much the entire school year. As much as I love teaching, it's just plain exhausting.

I was so tired one year that I started taking naps in my walk-in closet during my free periods. I would grab my yoga mat and coat for a pillow and blanket, lock the closet door, and pray no one was in my room when my alarm went off. Since I was pregnant at the time, I figured I had a pretty good excuse if anyone found out. Apparently, though, sleeping in the closet isn't as unusual as I thought, because I later found out that I wasn't the only teacher who had done this.

Whether or not you resort to drastic measures to make it through the day, I'm sure you are no stranger to the weariness that accompanies teaching. Exhaustion comes with the territory, but that doesn't mean we should resign ourselves to feeling like zombies all the time.

If we want to be effective, we need energy, and that means we need to take control of this area of our lives. Here are some thoughts to help you escape exhaustion:

1. **Take care of yourself.** Take naps, exercise, and drink water. When you're busy, you may feel like you don't have time for a nap. But twenty minutes of rest can refresh you and make you more focused and effective for the rest of the day. The same goes for exercising. Finding just a few minutes to exercise helps boost your energy, and even just going for a quick walk around the block can be invigorating.

2. **Make sure the students are the ones doing the work.** If you're standing in front of your class lecturing all day, you are doing all the work. You will be utterly exhausted, and your students probably won't be learning as much as they could because all they're doing is listening. Conserve energy and help your students learn better by giving more in-class work. Assign well-thought-out projects and activities that add value to your lesson, and spend more of your class time answering questions and helping students.

3. **Rely on God's strength.** When you have no strength left, God will give you what you need to make it through the day. He has promised to renew our strength (Isaiah 40:31) and that we can do all things through Him (Phil. 4:13). In fact, when we know we can't continue on our own, that's when we really see God's power. His strength is made perfect in our weakness (II Cor. 12:9-10). Pray, renew yourself in His Word, and rely on Him.

4. **Plan ahead.** My goal is always to have the entire next week's lessons, tests, and paperwork prepared by the time I leave school on Friday. This ensures that I stay ahead in my planning so that if something comes up (and don't we know something always comes up), I don't have to scramble at the

last minute. Having a cushion helps prevent unnecessary stress, which can zap our energy faster than anything. If this goal seems impossible, work over the weekend to have everything ready by Monday morning. (That's what I did my first year.)

Journal: How has weariness affected your teaching? What can you do to manage your fatigue and maintain the energy you need?

Lesson 47:
Keys to Communication

When I started teaching, I really didn't know what to say to parents. I was a rookie teacher, a newlywed with no children. What was I supposed to tell them at parent/teacher conferences? "Logan's doing great" or "Madeline needs to do her homework on time" was about the best I could think of.

But I knew that if I truly wanted to be effective, I needed to learn how to communicate with my students' parents. And even more importantly, how to develop meaningful relationships with them.

Here are a few things I have learned about communicating with parents:

1. **Have as much positive communication as possible.** Be intentional about sending home positive messages about your students. If parents already have two or three positive messages from you, they'll respond much better when you have to discuss a discipline issue.

2. **Send home more versus less.** Err on the side of too much communication instead of too little. If your school has an online system, post as much information there as possible. Email can also be a great way to send a lot of information without spending too much time (while also ensuring that

your letter doesn't die a slow death in the depths of your students' backpacks). When you notice an academic or behavioral problem, communicate with parents sooner rather than later. If you wait too long, the problem may have already mushroomed.

3. **Know when to pick up the phone.** Email is great, and I use it all the time. But sometimes a phone call or face-to-face conference is needed. If you find yourself writing a book of an email or wondering if the parent will be upset by your message, stop typing and pick up the phone. I also recommend a phone call whenever you have to administer significant discipline. That way you can inform the parents of the true story and get on the same page with them.

I had a student one year who was eating M&M's in class. After being told twice to put them away, she continued to pop the candy in her mouth. When I called her mom to inform her of the detention I had issued, the student had already told her mom that she got a detention for eating in class and "wasn't that so stupid." I'm glad I phoned the mom to let her know the detention was for disobedience, not just for eating candy.

4. **Provide customer service.** Whether your parents pay tuition or not, you should always try to provide great customer service. Do everything you can to make your school look good and help parents have a good experience.

5. Help parents think biblically. Sometimes you and a parent aren't able to get on the same page because the parent isn't thinking biblically. Maybe the parents don't think it's a big deal that their child told a lie or that their daughter is dressed immodestly. Instead of arguing or trying to defend the school's rules, humbly take the parents back to the Bible. Show them God's truth and allow the Holy Spirit to speak to their hearts. Remember that you are on the same team and both have the same goal – to help their child grow academically and spiritually.

6. Be humble. In all our interactions, we need to set aside our pride and display genuine humility. When we approach a conversation ready for a fight, a fight is most likely what we will get. But when we swallow our pride and lower our defenses, we allow God to work in and through us. Remember to seek first to understand the parent's concern. Don't get defensive and be prepared to adjust your position if necessary.

Journal: How can you better communicate with parents? What other lessons have you learned in this area? Share them on our discussion page at teach4theheart.com/discussions.

Lesson 48:
Ready, Aim, Fire!

"If you aim at nothing, you will hit it every time." This witticism by Zig Ziglar is as true for us as teachers as it is for our students. When you think of all that you hope to accomplish this year, you probably know you have a lot to aim for. But you need to be more intentional than that. You must set specific goals.

Setting goals is important because it focuses your efforts by giving you a definite target. I hope you have lots of things you are trying to accomplish, but try narrowing your focus to just a few main goals, no more than three to five. Of course you can still improve in other areas, but narrowing your focus will help you really grow in those key areas.

Try to make your goals specific and measurable. For example, "Be more organized" is not the best goal because it's too general to measure success. If becoming more organized is your overall goal, develop specific targets such as, "Make a to-do list each week" or "Create an organization system so that I do not lose a single student's paper this year." You're much more likely to actually accomplish these goals because you can see and measure your progress.

The best goals are both attainable and challenging. Unrealistic goals can lead to frustration, and goals that are easily attained result in little growth. Ask God to guide you as you set your objectives.

Once you have your goals set, plan time to reevaluate them and check your progress. Put a note in your calendar each month that says, "Evaluate goals." I love using a computerized calendar that sends me reminders (such as Microsoft Outlook), but use whatever method works well for you.

Then, go for it! Set up a system to help you accomplish your goals. Maybe you'll want to share your goals with a fellow teacher or your spouse. Not only can they keep you accountable, but they can also provide insight and ideas to help you along the way. And don't forget prayer; God is the most powerful Helper we have.

Put it into practice/Journal: Decide on a few specific, measurable goals. Then, develop a plan for accomplishing them.

Lesson 49:
Coast or Climb

I had just finished my third year of teaching and was sitting in our closing meeting thinking about how I finally had my classes down and didn't have that much to work on over the summer. Just then, our principal made an announcement. We would be starting a special writing initiative in which our students would write every day in every subject. We would all be studying and learning the methods over the summer and implementing them the next school year. *Well*, I thought, *I guess I have something to work on after all.*

And I'm so glad I did, because I was just about to get to the point where I might've started coasting through my teaching. I had figured out most of my problems and tweaked my curriculum. But when it felt like it was time to coast, it was actually time to climb, to learn something new and take my classroom to the next level. Some of you are still trying to keep your head above water (like I was my first couple years), but some of you have already mastered most areas of your classroom. In your case, it's time to climb to the next level.

Implementing writing to learn in your classroom will certainly improve your students' understanding, no matter what subject you teach. If you are ready to take this next step, check out the book *Content-Area Writing: Every Teacher's Guide* by Daniels, Zemelman, and Steineke. There's too much to say about the topic to do it justice in a few paragraphs, but this resource will tell you everything you need to know.

I would, however, like to give you a glimpse of what writing to learn is and why it's worth pursuing. Writing to learn means that your students write in ways that help them learn what they are studying. The writing is not formal and often not even graded, and the assignments can be as short or as long as you want. In my math class, I normally only spend about two minutes on these types of activities, but those two minutes are invaluable for helping students think more deeply and develop their writing skills.

Any question you would typically ask orally can be turned into a writing activity. When you do this, you engage every student because everyone must write an answer instead of just listening to the person who is called on.

You also get to know your students better by reading their writing. You'll be surprised how honest they'll be with you in their responses. As you incorporate writing into your daily routine, your students will become more and more comfortable with the skill. When it comes time to write a formal paper, they will be much less intimidated by the task.

For specific ideas of how to use writing to learn in your classroom, take a look at Appendix B.

Journal: Are you still growing as a teacher or have you started to coast? What steps will you take to ensure you continue to grow?

Lesson 50:
Not Just a Waste of Time

Our study together is coming to a close, but as we discussed in the last lesson, your learning should never stop. So are you ready for my suggestion for how you can keep learning?

Facebook, Twitter, and Pinterest.

Yes, you read correctly. While social media can become a black hole that wastes way too much of our day, it can also be a great tool to help you grow as a teacher.

It's all in the way you use social media. If you follow celebrities and share pictures of kittens, then, yes, you are probably just wasting your time. But if you are intentional about connecting with other great educators, you will find a constant stream of new ideas and resources. And all it really takes is 5-10 minutes a day.

Let's take a look at three major social media sites and how they can help you:

1. **Facebook**. You probably already use Facebook to connect with family and friends. So if you like some helpful pages and join a teachers' group, great teaching resources will automatically be added to your news feed. You'll start seeing them without even having to look.

2. **Twitter.** I recently started using Twitter, and I've been amazed by how many great ideas I've come across. If you're new to Twitter, set up an account and start following a few educators or educational blogs. Their latest thoughts and links to blog posts will show up in your feed.

3. **Pinterest.** I will admit I am just starting to use Pinterest myself, but I can already tell that the amount of ideas and resources compiled there is incredible. You can browse through images or choose to follow other educators or specific boards that you find helpful. Pinterest even has a section specifically for teachers. (See below.)

Don't be intimidated if you're not tech-savvy or if you don't know how to use these sites. Pick one to start with and ask a friend for a short introduction.

You'll be amazed at how much you'll learn.

Journal: How do you get new ideas for your classroom? Will social media be a good resource for you to take advantage of?

Put it into practice: If you're just beginning to use social media, here are some places you can start. Not all of these are Christian resources, so I wouldn't endorse everything they say. But I have found helpful articles from all these. The ones with asterisks are pages or groups with which I am affiliated.

Facebook:

>   Teach 4 the Heart:
>   www.facebook.com/DreamClassroom *

>   Christian Teachers' Lounge discussion group:
>   www.facebook.com/groups/ChristianTeachersTalk *

>   The Cornerstone for Teachers:
>   www.facebook.com/TheCornerstoneForTeachers

Twitter:

>   Me @LindaKardamis *

>   We Are Teachers @WeAreTeachers

>   Edutopia: @edutopia

Pinterest

>   Me: www.pinterest.com/lkardamis *

>   Teachers on Pinterest: www.pinterest.com/teachers

Back-to-School Power Pack

If the start of school is just around the corner, this is the place for you. The first weeks of school are absolutely essential because they set the tone for the entire year. You have the opportunity to reinvent your entire classroom culture, but you need to be ready. These lessons will help quickly prepare for your best start yet.

Power Pack Lessons:

Start by reading (or rereading) these lessons from the main section of the book:

> Whack a Mole? (Lesson 5)
>
> What's In a Name? (Lesson 6)
>
> Expect the Expected (Lesson 15)
>
> Practice Makes Perfect (Lesson 16)
>
> When the Bell Rings (Lesson 17)

Then continue on to these special back-to-school lessons:

> Welcome to Class (Lesson 51)
>
> Day One: Be Organized (Lesson 52)
>
> Day Two: Deal With the First Discipline Problem (Lesson 53)
>
> Please, No Déjà Vu! (Lesson 54)

Lesson 51:
Welcome to Class

During the first week of school, your class welcome sheet (or syllabus) should explain to your students and parents exactly what you expect of them. Having these expectations in writing provides students with a sense of security. Without this, conscientious students are often worried that they'll be blindsided by unforeseen expectations. Developing the class welcome sheet also helps you think through your policies.

Have the students and/or parents read and sign this form during the first week of school so that everyone is on the same page. This can even be the first homework assignment – a nice, easy way to start the year. If you have the capability to email parents, send them an electronic copy of your class welcome sheet.

As you develop your class welcome sheet, you may want consider the following sections (depending on your grade level and subject):

1. **Supplies**: What supplies should the students bring to school (elementary) or your class (secondary)? Is there a penalty for forgetting supplies?

2. **Homework**: Give students and parents an idea of the type and amount of homework to expect from your class. What will happen if homework is late?

3. **Class procedures:** Will you expect students to take notes? What other aspects of your class do parents and students need to know about?

4. **Tardiness:** What happens when a student is late to class or school?

5. **Absences:** How do students (or parents in lower grades) get make-up work following an absence?

6. **Grading system:** How will students' grades be calculated?

7. **Tips for success:** Write down a few tips to help your students succeed this year.

Discipline plan: What are your class rules? What are the penalties if a student chooses to break a rule? What rewards will be given for good behavior?

See Appendix D for an example of a class welcome sheet and discipline plan.

Put it into practice: Write or edit your class welcome sheet(s) for the upcoming year.

Lesson 52:
Day One: Be Organized

The first day of school sets the tone for the entire year, and your students will notice your confidence, organization, and classroom management skills right away. The key to a well-run first day of school is organization.

Plan every minute of the first day of school. What will you say to introduce yourself? How will you let students know where their seats are? How will you hand out textbooks? What material will you teach? How will you dismiss class? A well-thought-out plan will give you confidence and help the day run more smoothly.

Here are some suggestions for the first day of school:

1. **Have assigned seats.** Even if you plan to allow students to choose their seats at some point, assigning seats the first day of school shows that you are serious about having a well-managed classroom. It also helps you learn names more quickly. You could allow your students to sit where they want and then have everyone stand as you point out the new seats, but *The First Days of School* argues that this is a

disorganized and annoying way to start class. Instead, try one of these methods:

- *Have the students' names on their desks.* This works extremely well for self-contained classrooms but can also work well for first-period classes, as you can prepare this the night before. Simply write each student's name on his class welcome sheet and put it on his desk.

- *Number the seats.* Place a number on each desk. Then let the students know their numbers immediately upon entering the room. You can write their names and numbers on a handout, poster, transparency, or smart board. They could be listed in alphabetical order or on a seating chart. (I highly recommend numbering seats, even if you're displaying a seating chart. Students get confused trying to figure out which side is left and right or front and back on a seating chart, even if you label it. The last thing you want is for half the class to be lost.)

2. **Have all textbooks ready to pass out.** Don't distribute textbooks from your closet. The method works, but having textbooks out and ready conveys organization and competence. You could call each student to the front to receive his book, but you are wasting time. Try to think of how you can accomplish these tasks most smoothly and efficiently. Your students will notice. I count mine out and put them at the end of each row by the wall. When it comes time to pass them out, I instruct students where to find each stack and how to pass them down the row. Even better is to have them on the students' desks when they enter the room, but that is not always possible if you have classes back-to-back.

3. **Go over *some* rules and expectations**. Hand out you class welcome sheet and hit a few highlights, but don't go over the entire handout. It's very boring for students to hear class rules the entire day. Plus, they can read them on their own. Instead, discuss only what the students need to know for the first day. Then, go over the rest of the expectations as they come up. (For example, explain homework procedures the first day you assign homework.) I require my students to read and sign the class welcome sheet and discipline plan for homework the first night.

4. **Teach something**. While there are lots of procedures to go over the first day of school, make every effort to actually teach for at least five to ten minutes of each class period or subject. This shows the students that you're serious about learning and want to get right to work. Plus, most students will actually appreciate a break from hearing about procedures, policies, and fire drill exits all day.

Don't stop here; keep thinking. How will you dismiss the students? How will you run restroom breaks? How will you introduce yourself? The time you put into planning will be well worth it when your first day is the smoothest you've ever had.

Journal: Think through all of the details of the first day of school. How will you accomplish each task you have planned?

Lesson 53:
Day Two: Deal with the First Discipline Problem

If you're organized, day one normally goes fairly smoothly. You may even make it through the entire day without a single discipline issue, especially if you have a new group of students each class period. By the second day, however, your first behavioral problem will present itself, and you need to be ready.

We discussed in Lesson 5 how vital it is to deal with issues while they are still small. This is the time to put that knowledge into action. Watch for the first misbehavior in your students and address it immediately. Remember, don't yell at the student or make him feel stupid, but you must correct every small problem. Kindly say something like, "Katelyn, please sit up and pay attention. I know you may be tired, but you are not allowed to put your head on your desk. Thank you." Once you've caught the first one, you can mentally give yourself a pat on the back, but don't lower your guard. Get ready for the next situation. Maintain absolute vigilance for at least the first two weeks.

Why do you have to be so vigilant at the start of school? Because you are setting the tone for the entire year. If you deal with every small problem the first two weeks, your students will quickly rise to meet your expectations. You will still have to deal with issues for the rest of the year, but they should remain small if you set high expectations from day one. If you don't deal with these little problems now, you will likely find yourself with an out-of-control classroom within a few months. And when that happens, it's extremely difficult to bring the class back under control.

Remember, you can always relax your expectations later. If you find that a certain class is normally very diligent, you can allow a little more freedom because they have learned where the boundary is. If you start with freedom, however, students will resent the boundaries you later impose.

One final note: Please be kind to your students as you address these issues. The students are learning your system, and you do not want to embarrass them. This is not the time to show you're the boss by coming down hard. Unless you have a major attitude problem right away, you shouldn't need to dispense any punishments the first few days of school. Instead, address each issue with compassion, remembering that you're simply teaching what acceptable behavior looks like in your classroom. Remember the Golden Rule: Treat the students how you would want to be treated.

Journal: How will you handle the first discipline problem that arises? If you're nervous, write out exactly what you will say to small issues such as talking, running into class, not paying attention, and getting up without permission. Practice your response in front of the mirror or to a friend.

Lesson 54:
Please, No Déjà Vu!

After a rough start to my teaching career, I spent my first summer preparing for a vastly different second year. Even though I felt ready for my fresh start, I did have one concern: I was going to face some of the same students I'd had the year before. They would expect to be able to act the same way, and I knew I would have to quickly show them differently.

If you are planning big changes to your classroom this year but will have some of the same challenging students, you need to be ready. Your new classroom starts on day one.

Typically, the first day of school doesn't bring many discipline issues. Most of the students are just absorbing the newness and gauging their teachers and will start to test your resolve over the next few days. However, this may not be the case for students that you've previously allowed too much freedom. They may walk into your classroom already wound up to be in a class where they think they can push the teacher around. This is exactly how two of my previously unruly students started my pre-algebra class the first day of school. They ran into the room laughing and started cracking jokes the moment the bell rang.

My job was to show them immediately that things would be different, and that will be your job as well. I knew the answer was not to yell at them right away. Instead, I kindly but firmly dealt with each misbehavior. I started by simply informing them that their actions were not acceptable. Since I addressed even small misconducts, they got the idea pretty quickly that I meant business. I was, however, prepared to follow through with discipline measures if my verbal correction had not been enough.

Although you must be prepared to address issues right away, don't get psyched up for a fight. You are getting a fresh start, and you should allow your students a fresh start as well. Don't hold their past behavior against them. However, if you do experience a major attitude problem on day one, be ready to pull that student aside and speak with him about your expectations for the new year. If a student really chooses to push you, you may need to discipline right away. Have discernment. Try to be as kind and forgiving as possible, but don't allow any misbehavior to go uncorrected and be mentally prepared in case a situation escalates.

Finally, pray specifically for the students that make you most nervous. Pray that God will work in their hearts and that He will give you wisdom and the right words.

Journal: If you will have some of the same students again, how will you handle discipline with kindness but firmness? Do you need to seek another teacher's wisdom for any particular situation? If so, ask a fellow teacher today or post your question online in Christian Teachers' Lounge.

Epilogue:
Onward We Go

While we all know how challenging teaching can be, we also know that helping students grow is incredibly rewarding. If it's your first year teaching, I want you to know that it gets a whole lot easier – as long as you continue to learn and grow.

I pray this book has been a help and encouragement to you. But don't let the journey stop here. We can all continue to grow as we share ideas, resources, personal stories, and encouragement. That's where Teach 4 the Heart comes in. It started as simply a way to spread the word about this book but it's grown into so much more. It's now a vibrant community of Christian teachers & a place where I can continue to provide encouragement, inspiration, and ideas. We would love to have you, and you can join for free at teach4theheart.com.

Also, if you already done so, be sure to check out the special *Create Your Dream Classroom* bonuses. These include printable versions of discipline essays and welcome sheets as well as additional articles, links to our discussion groups, and much more.

Visit teach4theheart.com/bonuses to grab your bonuses & find out more about Teach 4 the Heart.

I look forward to continuing to connect with you via Teach 4 the Heart. In the meantime, if I can help in any way, please contact me. I would love to hear from you. Any feedback, suggestions, or personal stories are also welcomed.

Appendix A:
Course Calendar Plans

This calendar will help you schedule each chapter (and if you're going to be more detailed, each lesson) throughout the year.

Step 1: If you are not already familiar with the course, examine the course, textbooks, and any major projects that the course will include.

Step 2: Look at your school's calendar for the year and figure out how many days of class you will have. If you don't have time to count each day, you can probably estimate around 170 (or 42 per quarter if you're in the middle of the year), but if you're able to be more accurate that's even better. Estimate how many classes you'll lose to field trips, practices, half days, standardized testing, etc.

Step 3: Divide the number of days remaining by the number of chapters you have left. This will provide you with a very rough estimate of the days per chapter.

If you know you're not going to have time to finish all the chapters in your curriculum, don't just give up on the last chapter. Strategically plan which chapter is least critical and make that the one you skip.

Step 4: (Optional but recommended) The more accurate you can be with your plan, the better, so work through each chapter, shortening or lengthening the number of days allowed for each. Plan which lessons you may skip if needed. If this is your first time mapping the course, don't stress too much. Just make an educated guess. Next summer, you can fine-tune your plan.

Step 5: Set up a calendar. The simplest way to do this is to first mark off the days when you will not have class. Then, start counting out the days for each chapter. For example, if you planned 16 days for a chapter, count 16 days and write "Chapter Test" on the 16th day. Continue through the rest of the year. Finally, format your plan however you like. Leave it as a calendar or make it into a list of chapter end dates.

Feel free to plan in more detail. I plan which section of each chapter I will teach on each day and which ones I will spend extra time on. This helps me know exactly how many days behind or ahead I am at any point in the school year.

Appendix B:
Writing to Learn

The following writing-to-learn activities will light up your classroom. To learn more about this topic, read *Content-Area Writing: Every Teacher's Guide* by Harvey Daniels, Steven Zemelman, and Nancy Steineke.

1. **Exit Slip.** During the last two or three minutes of class, students answer a question and drop it off on their way out the door. Prompts can range from questions from the day's lesson to general questions such as these:

   1) What is the most important thing you learned in class today?

   2) How would you explain this concept to a friend?

   3) Did you understand today's lesson? Why or why not?

   4) What questions do you have about today's lesson?

   5) How well are you understanding this chapter? What can I do to help?

   6) What do you need to do to prepare for our upcoming test?

2. **Written Questions.** Students write down the answer to a question about the lesson. For example, ask a question like, "How do you find the direct object of a sentence?" Instead of taking an oral response, have each student write his answer on a sheet of paper or in his notes.

3. **Writing Break.** At any point in the lesson, students pause and write for a given length of time (one to five minutes). You can tell them to write what they've learned or you can give them a specific prompt. All students must write for the entire time.

4. **Answer Explanation.** Students explain how they found an answer. In math class, ask students to write the steps they used to solve a problem. For studies such as literature or science, asking students to explain how they determined the answer helps them give a more complete response.

5. **Error Analysis.** Students figure out why they got an answer wrong and what they should have done. This is best used in skill subjects such as math and grammar but can work well in other subjects too.

6. **My Thoughts.** Students have a section of their notes called "my thoughts" in which they record their thoughts (as opposed to just copying the notes you provide).

7. **Write a Quiz:** Students write a five-question quiz over the material. They then exchange and take another student's quiz. Students grade the quiz that they wrote and discuss the correct answers with the one who took their quiz.

8. **Admit Slip.** Similar to an exit slip, an admit slip is due when the student enters class (or can be done right at the start of class). Students answer a question or respond to a prompt.

9. **Written Conversation.** Students write back and forth to each other. Be sure to give good prompts to ensure that the conversations are valuable and contribute to learning.

10. **Reflective Write**. Students reflect on how they are learning, what would help them learn better, how far they have come, etc.

11. **Student/Teacher Correspondence.** Your students write you a letter about whatever they want. You can then either respond with short notes on their papers or you can make comments orally in class.

*Many of these ideas are derived from *Content-Area Writing: Every Teacher's Guide* by Harvey Daniels, Steven Zemelman, and Nancy Steineke.

Appendix C:
Discipline Essays

Below are examples of discipline essays, both pre-written essays that students simply copy and essays consisting of questions that students answer. Feel free to use these as they are written or to rework them to fit your situation.

For your convenience, digital copies are also available for download at teach4theheart.com/bonuses

Part 1: Question-Directed Essays

Essay – Disrupting Class
(Talking or other disruptions)

Name: _____

Due: _____

Please complete the following essay in complete sentences on separate sheets of paper and staple them behind this page. Discuss your answers with your parents, and have one of them sign below.

Parent's signature: _____

**Please note: This essay is meant to help you reflect on how disrupting class affects you and those around you. Use this time to reevaluate your actions and determine to behave appropriately in the future.

1. Copy the following verses from the Bible on a separate sheet of paper: Philippians 2:4, I Corinthians 14:40, Hebrews 13:17, Colossians 3:23

2. Write at least two sentences for each verse explaining how it relates to disrupting class.

3. Write a paragraph (at least five sentences) applying the principles from the verses above to this specific situation. In other words, what does the Bible have to say about your disrupting class today?

4. Write a paragraph (at least five sentences) explaining why disrupting class is harmful to you, your classmates and your teacher.

5. Write a paragraph (at least five sentences) giving a plan of action for how you will avoid being disruptive in the future.

Essay – Diligence in Class
(Not completing work or lack of effort)

Name: _____

Due: _____

Please complete the following essay in complete sentences on separate sheets of paper and staple them behind this page. Discuss your answers with your parents, and have one of them sign below.

Parent's signature: _____

**Please note: This essay is meant to help you reflect on God's view of diligence. Use this time to reevaluate your actions and determine to put forth better effort in the future.

1. Copy the following verses from the Bible on a separate sheet of paper: Colossians 3:23, Proverbs 10:4, Proverbs 22:29, Proverbs 12:24

2. Write at least two sentences for each verse describing how it relates to school work.

3. Write a paragraph (at least five sentences) applying the principles from the verses above to this specific situation. In other words, what does God expect from you as a student?

4. Write a paragraph (at least five sentences) explaining why you have not been giving your best effort.

5. Write a paragraph (at least five sentences) discussing why working hard is beneficial for you.

6. Write a paragraph (at least five sentences) giving a specific plan of action for how you will be more diligent in the future.

Essay - Friendship

Name: _____

Due: _____

Please complete the following essay in complete sentences on separate sheets of paper and staple them behind this page. Discuss your answers with your parents, and have one of them sign below.

Parent's signature: _____

**Please note: This essay is about you and how you can be a better friend. It is not about the mistakes your friend has made. The Bible teaches that we are each responsible for our own actions and should not push blame on other people, especially our friends. As you complete this essay, try not to worry about your friend's mistakes. Instead, focus on how you can be better, and let your friend worry about what he or she needs to change.

1. Copy the following verses from the Bible on a separate sheet of paper: Proverbs 16:28, Matthew 7:12, Proverbs 27:10a, Ephesians 4:29-32, Romans 12:10

2. Write a paragraph (at least five sentences) explaining what these verses say about friendship.

3. Write a paragraph (at least five sentences) describing the ways in which you have failed to be a good friend in the past.

4. Write a paragraph (at least five sentences) detailing specific ways you can be a better friend in the future.

5. List at least ten good character traits of your friend. Think about why you are friends with him or her in the first place.

6. Write a letter to your friend (at least eight sentences) on a different sheet of paper telling him or her what you learned while doing this essay and how you want to treat him or her in the future.

Part II: Pre-Written Essays

Pre-written Essay: Talking without permission

Unwarranted talking in class is a selfish act for many reasons. If it is a time of instruction, talking is a disruption to others and a distraction to the teacher. When I talk, I rob my classmates of the opportunity to receive instruction unhindered. Unauthorized talking is disrespectful to the teacher who has spent time preparing the lesson. Talking also causes me to miss valuable instruction and often makes the teacher repeat the material. If I talk during a time allowed for individual work, I create a distraction and disrupt the thought process of others. I cannot be focused on my own work if I am talking. Talking without permission is inconsiderate and implies that I am more important than everyone else in the room. This is contrary to Scripture which admonishes, "Look not every man on his own things, but every man also on the things of others." (Philippians 2:4) Therefore, I will not talk in class without permission.

*Special thanks to Bernadette Bileci for contributing this essay.

Pre-written Essay: Being unkind to fellow students

I must always be kind, loving, and considerate to others. Ephesians 4:32 teaches, "And be ye kind one to another, tenderhearted, forgiving one another, even as God for Christ's sake hath forgiven you." While it is easy to make fun of someone, this is not being kind and loving. Jesus said in John 13:34-35, "A new commandment I give unto you, That ye love one another; as I have loved you, that ye also love one another. By this shall all men know that ye are my disciples, if ye have love one to another." Loving one another is our highest calling as Christians, and when I put someone else down, I am forsaking this high calling. While this commandment is not easy to live out, I should try every day with God's help to be more loving.

Even when someone is unkind or mean to me, I should still love them as I Peter 3:8-9 teaches: "Finally, be ye all of one mind, having compassion one of another, love as brethren, be pitiful, be courteous: Not rendering evil for evil, or railing for railing: but contrariwise blessing; knowing that ye are thereunto called, that ye should inherit a blessing." When I am kind to others and love and forgive them as Christ loves and forgives me, I show true biblical Christianity and inherit the blessings that come from pleasing the Savior.

Pre-written Essay: Silliness or distracting other students

When I am in class I should not distract others by silliness or other means. Class time is a time to learn and receive instruction. When I am acting silly, I not only keep myself from learning, but also distract other students who are trying to learn. I am a disruption to the class and a distraction to the teacher. By being silly, I'm robbing classmates of the opportunity to receive instruction unhindered. Distractions also cause one to miss valuable instruction and often necessitate repeated material. If I am distracting during a time allowed for individual work, I'm interrupting the thought processes of others. Neither my classmates nor I can be focused on our own work if I am being silly. Distracting others is inconsiderate and implies that I am more important than everyone else in the room. This is contrary to Scripture, which admonishes, "Look not every man on his own things, but every man also on the things of others." Philippians 2:4. Therefore, I will strive to not be silly in class or be a distraction to others.

Pre-written Essay: Working during class work times

I will use my class time to work on tasks I am given. I must take notes and work problems and not read a book, write notes, or work on something else. To disregard a teacher's instructions is disobedience, and if I chose to continue to not apply myself to completing assignments, I am disobeying and will receive a detention. The Bible teaches that I am to do my best in all things and to work diligently. Colossians 3:23 teaches, "And whatsoever ye do, do it heartily, as to the Lord, and not unto men;" When I am in class, I am to work diligently for the Lord and apply myself wholeheartedly to my education. If I am reading a book, writing notes, or working on something else, I am not diligently learning. I must realize that God desires to reward diligence as He states in Proverbs 10:4, "He who has a slack hand becomes poor, but the hand of the diligent makes rich." Therefore, I must work hard in class to complete the work I am given.

Pre-written Essay: Talking during a fire drill

While talking during a fire drill may not seem like a big deal, it is actually an important matter of safety. In the event of an emergency, students need to be quiet and act orderly in order to be able to hear important instructions from teachers or administration. If I am being disruptive and loud, I could actually prevent myself and others from hearing important instructions about how to get to safety. While the teacher is taking roll, we must stand quietly and answer quickly in case a student is missing in the building. In the event of an emergency, the teacher needs to locate any missing students extremely quickly in order to make sure everyone is safely out of the building. The purpose of fire drills is to practice and prepare so that everyone is prepared in the event of a true emergency. Therefore, I must follow all emergency procedures at all time, including staying under control and quiet to ensure the safety of myself and others. In the future, I must have self-control and keep in mind the true purpose of fire drills.

Appendix D:
Sample Class Welcome Sheet
& Discipline Plan

Welcome to Pre-Algebra

We have an exciting year ahead of us! In order to make our class time more enjoyable and educational for each of you, I'd like to explain some of my procedures and expectations.

CLASSROOM POLICIES:

Supplies: *To be brought to class EVERY DAY.*

1. Textbook (covered)

2. Math notes (composition notebook)

3. Math folder containing blank paper

4. Student planner

5. Pencil and green pen

6. You will also occasionally need a scientific calculator or graph paper. I will let you know in advance when these are needed.

When any of these supplies are missing, you will receive an unprepared. After the 3rd, 4th, and 5th unprepared, you will be required to complete an assignment in a teacher's room during lunch. The 6th unprepared will result in a detention. This starts over each quarter.

Homework

Do your best on each assignment. In math, doing your homework correctly is vital for your success in mastering the concepts. Therefore, the following procedures will apply:

1. **Complete every homework problem** to the best of your ability. Never leave a problem blank. Consult your notes or ask someone for help if you are confused.

2. **Write down the original problem.**

3. **Show your work.**

4. **Circle your answers.**

5. **Use pencil.**

6. **Only use a calculator when necessary**. When the numbers get large, you may use a calculator. Write *C* next to the problem to indicate you used a calculator.

7. You may (and should) ask another student or a parent for help about *how* to work a problem. They may give you hints, guide you through the problem, or check your work to help you locate mistakes. However, if you copy another person's homework or allow someone to give you an answer without working it out on your own, you are cheating.

60-70% of your homework grade will be based on how much effort you put into each problem. If you do not follow these directions, you may be required to redo your homework.

Notes

Each student will keep a composition notebook of math notes. These will provide procedures and examples of how to solve problems and should be used when completing homework and studying. These notes will be collected and graded the day of each test.

Late Work

With the exception of unplanned absences, **all work must be turned in on time.** When a homework assignment is not completed on time, it must be turned in the following day to receive any partial credit that is available. See the student handbook for more details regarding partial credit. **Habitually turning in work late is not acceptable.**

Tardiness

1. If you are late because you were needed by a teacher or staff member, you must bring a pass from that teacher/staff member in order to be excused.

2. When you enter the classroom late (with or without a pass), enter so as not to distract the rest of the class. Silently enter the room, hand the teacher your pass, and join the rest of the class in our activity.

3. Three unexcused tardies in any quarter will result in a detention.

Absence

When you are absent, **you are responsible to make up all the work you missed.**

1. Check the absent folder to see what you missed.

2. Copy the notes you missed from a friend.

3. Make up any homework assignments you missed as soon as possible.

4. Make up any tests/quizzes you missed.

*Note: If an assignment was due the day you were absent, it must be turned in the first day you return.

Grading – points system (Percentages are estimates that may vary depending on the number of assignments.)

Tests: 100 points each   (around 45%)

Quizzes: 20 points each   (around 24%)

Homework: 5 points each   (around 20%)

Class work: 2-5 points each   (around 6%)

Notes: 10 points each   (around 5%)

FINAL NOTES:

Math is an incredible subject in which we study the orderly rules God placed into our universe. I love mathematics and hope to help you will enjoy it as well. The key to success in math is to do your very best on each homework assignment. If you are struggling at any time, please come see me. The concepts build upon each other, and I don't want anyone to get behind. Let's have a great year and honor God in all we do.

"Not with eyeservice, as men-pleasers, but as bondservants of Christ, doing the will of God from the heart, with goodwill doing service, as to the Lord, and not to men, knowing that whatever good anyone does, he will receive the same from the Lord."

– Ephesians 6:6-8a

Please feel free to contact me at any time.
Email: teacher@school.edu
School number: 888-888-8888

STUDENTS: I have read these classroom procedures and understand that I am responsible for following them.

Signature _____

PARENTS: I have read and am aware of these classroom procedures.

Signature _____

PLEASE KEEP THIS SHEET IN YOUR FOLDER AT ALL TIMES.

Thank you.

Discipline Plan for Room 260
Classroom Rules

1. Communicate with others only when given permission.

2. Stay in your seat unless given permission.

3. Participate in all classroom activities (Colossians 3:23).

4. Be respectful and kind to others (Ephesians 4:32).

If You Choose to Break a Rule

Students who choose to communicate with others or get out of their seat without permission will be given a warning. Any student who receives three warnings in one day will be given a writing assignment.

Students who choose to distract others or not participate in class activities, including reading, working on other materials or writing notes, will be given a writing assignment. No warnings will be given.

Students who choose to be unkind to another student in any way will be given a writing assignment. No warnings will be given.

Continued or flagrant violations will result in a detention.

If You Earn a Writing Assignment

Writing assignments are due at the beginning of class the following day and must contain a parent/guardian's signature.

If the assignment is not turned in at the beginning of class the next day with a parent/guardian's signature, the student will be required to work on the assignment during lunch in a teacher's room. The assignment may also be doubled.

If the complete assignment is still not turned in at the beginning of class the next day with a parent/guardian's signature, the student will receive a detention.

Rewards

Praise

Positive notes home

Free seating days

Student of the month

An orderly, safe, and productive learning environment

STUDENTS: I have read this classroom discipline plan and understand it. I will honor it while in Room 260.

Signature _____

PARENTS: My child has discussed this discipline plan with me. I understand it and will support it.

Signature _____

TEACHER: I will strive to be fair and consistent in administering the discipline plan for Room 260.

Signature _____

PLEASE KEEP THIS SHEET IN YOUR FOLDER AT ALL TIMES.

Thank you.

This discipline plan is modeled after a sample found in *The First Days of School* by Harry and Rosemary Wong, p. 160.

Suggested Resources

Content-Area Writing: Every Teacher's Guide by Harvey Daniels, Steven Zemelman, and Nancy Steineke
>A handbook for incorporating writing into your classroom

The First Days of School: How to Be an Effective Teacher by Harry & Rosemary Wong
>A wealth of detailed advice on conducting an orderly, effective classroom

The Seven Habits of Highly Effective People by Stephen Covey
>Seven powerful principles that will transform your classroom and life

Shepherding a Child's Heart by Tedd Tripp
>An encouragement to disciple the heart

Understanding the Times by David Noebel
>A discussion of various worldviews

The Universe Next Door: A Basic Worldview Catalog by James W. Sire
>A discussion of various worldviews

Your Reactions Are Showing by J. Allan Peterson
>A pamphlet discussing appropriate reactions

Get Your Bonuses!
teach4theheart.com/bonuses

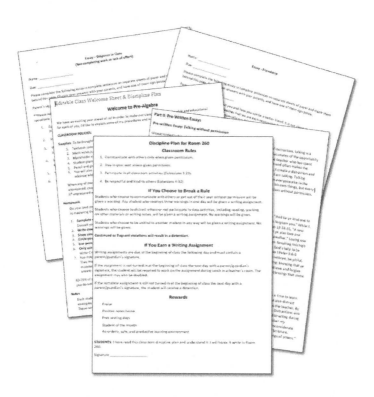

Download printable versions of class welcome sheets, discipline plans, discipline essays and more.